MARSHA TOM

NAIL THAT JOB!

NAVIGATING THE JOB SEARCH JUNGLE

Headshot by Gabyhendry.com

ISBN: 979-8-9901958-1-3 Paperback

ACKNOWLEDGEMENTS

Profoundly grateful falls short in expressing my appreciation to the many friends and my family over the years who have encouraged me in my walk with God to discover and pursue my purpose. To all my wonderful mentees on both coasts, I have had the honor and privilege of guiding, teaching, and living life with you, as you have brought me some of my greatest joy. Thank you for your precious trust. I am so grateful you also encouraged and inspired me in each of your unique ways. This handbook serves as a testimony to friendship, where knowledge, trust, and wisdom flow both ways.

A special heaping of love and gratitude to Adrien, Anthuan, and Hannah for withstanding my relentless questioning and requests for help and listening to even my doubts and fears as this handbook evolved to serve others with the best I have to offer.

All of you, my dear friends, far and near and around the globe, are so precious to me. I learned much from each of you.

CONTENTS

Introduction: How to Use This Handbook xi

Preparing Your Heart

1   When Is the Right Time to Search for a Job? 1
2   What Does Your Job-Seeker State of Mind
    Tell Others? 7
3   The Heart's Echo: Living in a State of Gratitude 13
4   Hope: Trusting the Plan for Your Career 19

Let's Get Started!

5   Through Thick and Thin: The Buddy System 29
6   Ya Gotta Do Your Homework 35
7   Showcasing Your Value: Crafting a Results-
    Driven Resume...41
8   Harnessing Humility: The Cornerstone to
    Interview Mastery 47

In the Thick of It

9   Seeing from the Employer's Perspective 55
10   Charting the Interview Journey..................................61
11   The Famous First and Scariest Question 69

12 Strategic Storytelling: Mastering the
    P-A-R-T Technique.. 77
13 The Two-Way Street of Interviews.............................85
14 Individual and Panel Interviews: A Dance
    of Discernment..95
15 Mastering the Digital Handshake:
    Succeeding in Virtual Interviews.......................... 103
16 Questions That Get the Employer Excited 111
17 The Art of Post-Interview Gratitude........................ 119
18 So, You Applied for the Same Job Twice, Huh? 125

Now, We Wait and Pray

19 The Power of Prayer in Your Career Journey 133
20 Navigating the Wait with Grace and Strategy.......... 141
21 Please Don't Call the Employer to Ask If
    You Got the Job 149
22 Anchored by Community: Construct
    Your Support System 157

Finishing It All Up

23 Curating a Positive Social Media Presence............... 165
24 Overcoming Fear 171
25 Learning Zones: The Growth Beyond Comfort 179
26 Resilience: Rising After Rejection........................187
27 Embracing the Bounce: A Stepping Stone
    to Success 197
28 The Gift of Service: Unemployment as a
    Time for Growth.. 205

29 At the Crossroads: Is it Time to Leave Your Job? 213

30 Compassion: The Value of Volunteering
in Times of Transition 221

A Final Word 227
About the Author 235

MY HOPE FOR YOU

Thank you for entrusting me with your professional development through this handbook, *Nail That Job, Navigating the Job Search Jungle*. My hope is it becomes an invaluable resource to you, offering both practical steps and spiritual encouragement for your journey ahead.

I have poured prayer over all the chapters in hopes each one gives you guidance and wisdom and highlights opportunities you recognize for self-growth. For those who are discouraged, God will lift your spirits and rekindle your hope. God is your ever-present source of comfort and support, especially during weak moments. If you have given up, God can reignite your determination and fill you with renewed purpose. And for those of you who are excited and ready to embrace new opportunities, God will bless your efforts if you look to him with your trust. Know that God works behind the scenes for your good, helping you to weave your stories and experiences together as you seek to find your purpose through a career opportunity.

Heavenly Father, I lift up to you, the person reading these words. I come to you with a humble heart, seeking your guidance, wisdom, and knowledge for all those who are on the journey of discovering their career through the purpose you have designed for them. In times of uncertainty, give them strength to persevere, knowing that your divine plan is unfolding, even when it's unseen. Thank you for being with each reader through every step of the process.

INTRODUCTION:
HOW TO USE THIS HANDBOOK

In a world that often seems to prioritize success as measured by material wealth and titles, there lies a deeper calling that beckons each of us to discover not just who we are but who we are meant to be. This handbook is an invitation to embark on a voyage of discovery, one that goes beyond the resume, job titles, and office walls to the very essence of what it means to live a life of purpose and faith. At the heart of our lives lies a quest for meaning, for purpose, and for fulfillment that transcends the mundane tasks of daily life.

I've learned that any pain you face in life is a lesson that can be used for someone else's benefit. No pain should ever be wasted without a purposeful end. This is what led me to create *Nail That Job!* I want everyone to know how to avoid the pain of discouragement and the lie of unworthiness that plagues us when we can't secure a job we love and think is perfect for us.

In these pages, you will find not just strategies for navigating the professional world but also, and more importantly, guidance for aligning your career path with your deepest convictions and values. It is a journey that acknowledges the complexities of living in the modern world while striving to remain faithful to one's spiritual compass. Through personal stories, practical advice, and reflective insights, this handbook aims to guide you toward a career that not only sustains you financially but also enriches your soul and contributes to a greater good.

Your best approach to this handbook is to engage with it from beginning to end. As you embark on the comprehensive journey from self-discovery to expressing gratitude post-interview, the narrative will unfold most coherently. Along the way, you'll find QR codes for scanning—think of these as little gateways, opening up to further resources like free worksheets and templates that are ready to assist in enhancing your outcomes.

Of course, the beauty of *Nail That Job* is its adaptability. Each chapter is designed for you to quickly pinpoint and absorb the knowledge relevant to your immediate needs without requiring a full read-through. I encourage you to utilize the Table of Contents as your navigational tool. Are you curious about the right questions to ask a prospective employer during an interview? Skip ahead to Chapter 16. Looking for insights on how to perceive and answer questions from an employer's viewpoint? Chapter 9 awaits.

Whatever chapter you find yourself in, know that this journey you're on is being navigated with divine intention. My website, marshatom.com, is there for additional guidance or if you seek a more personal coaching experience with me.

Using my handbook, you will discover that a great deal of psychology is used, and you will need to change your perspective. Do the work, and you will see the change in yourself. It happens with every client I coach. *Nail That Job!* is designed with intentionality so you can read any chapter and work on a specific skill. Changing what you give out during an interview doesn't happen until there is change within. As one of my chapters says, do your homework. It's a handbook that teaches; it's not a book designed to entertain. I'm all about learning and growing, and that's what you will gain.

No matter how you engage with this handbook, my prayer is you will discover your God-given purpose and pursue it with the support you'll glean from these pages. Let this book be a companion as you navigate the crossroads of career and faith, helping you to discern not only the next steps on your professional journey but also how they can lead you to a fuller, more meaningful existence. In blending the practical with the spiritual, we embark together on a path that seeks not just success in the conventional sense but a deeper satisfaction that comes from living in accordance with one's faith and values. Welcome to a journey of discovery, purpose, and faith.

PREPARING YOUR HEART

WHEN IS THE RIGHT TIME TO SEARCH FOR A JOB?

Keep faith amidst uncertainty and focus on your calling rather than the storm around you.

You are getting laid off. Quick! It's time to look for a job. Most people will search for the next position when they are no longer employed. In actuality, it's better to always keep an eye on the potential job market and your positioning in any season. Have you been ignoring signs it was time to move on? If you find yourself training everyone and no one is training you, it means you have probably outgrown the position. If the fire of challenge is lost and has fizzled, it's time to get it back. Be aware if you are just surviving in a toxic environment. The best time to look for a job is when you have a job. Remember this advice. Employers are prone to hire employed people over unemployed people.

Let's delve into the heart of job searching, an endeavor that transcends the mere act of finding employment. It's about aligning one's vocation with one's divine calling. As you journey, expect to uncover not only the practicalities of job searching but also how to intertwine your faith and hopes with your career aspirations, allowing for a harmonious blend that leads to both professional fulfillment and spiritual growth. Understanding your calling helps you define the purpose you were designed for so you can move toward a fulfilling career.

The job search can often feel like you're barely treading water while sailing against the current. There was a time I found myself drifting in this very situation when I didn't prepare for what might happen. During the recession of 2008, each resume sent felt like a message in a bottle just bobbing along in the ocean. But it was during these moments I was reminded of the story of Peter walking on water toward Jesus. The moment Peter took his focus off him, he sank. *"Keep faith amidst uncertainty and focus on your calling rather than the storm around you."* The storm is temporary; your calling is not.

When we search for a job, we're also searching for a purpose. It's not just about the paycheck at the end of the month but finding a place where our skills and talents meet the needs of the world. In life, we are called to be stewards of the gifts we've been given, using them not just for our benefit but for the greater good. It's so important for you to understand your worth beyond a title. Every individual is more than a job title. In the training I've taught, I emphasize our worth is not tied to our employment status; rather, it's rooted in who created us.

It may be time for you to find that new position that challenges you to grow. You are not meant to stop growing and become stagnant. At times, if you stay too long in the same position, a door is opened and helps to give you the firm boot you need so that you can move on to what is in store for you, which is even bigger and better than what you thought was possible. My hope is that while you are waiting, you are navigating potential rejection with grace. God is probably redirecting you without you realizing it. I've learned, sometimes through tears, that every 'no' from an employer is a step toward the 'yes' where I'm meant to be. Trust that you are being led to the place you are supposed to be. Just realize there may be stepping stones you have to endure before you get there.

In the heavy space between jobs, when you feel discouraged, know this is fertile ground for growth. I encourage you to learn, volunteer, and expand your horizons, as these experiences will enrich your professional narrative and bring you hope. Don't be caught off guard. It's important for you to be proactive and take the necessary steps about your career so you can avoid becoming reactive to what the world offers you.

PRAYER POINTS

1. Pray for discernment and wisdom in your job search.
2. Pray for peace in the face of rejection, knowing it's part of a larger plan.
3. Pray for opportunities that align with your God-given purpose.

CALL-TO-ACTION

Today, take a step to refine one aspect of your job search process, whether it's updating your resume, reaching out for networking, or simply spending time in prayer for guidance. Pick up your toolbox of skills and accept the next challenge so you can keep growing and sharing with others the gifts God has given you. We often live with expectancy and perfection and have forgotten God wants us to live our lives helping each other and lifting each other up. We were created with gifts to help others and not help ourselves.

Apostle Paul shared his concerns in his letter to the Galatians about the need for Jews and Gentiles alike to serve and love each other. Let's remember while searching for the right job, we need to focus on the importance of helping others while doing what we need to do to help ourselves.

> "Each one should test their own actions. Then they can take pride in themselves alone, without comparing themselves to someone else, for each one should carry their own load."
> Galatians 6:4–5 (NIV)

CLOSING PRAYER

Heavenly Father, as we navigate the waters of career decisions, may we be anchored in your wisdom and guided by your light. Grant us the courage to pursue our calling with faith, trusting that you are with us at every turn.

MY TAKE AWAYS

_____

_____

_____

_____

_____

_____

_____

_____

_____

_____

_____

_____

_____

WHAT DOES YOUR JOB-SEEKER STATE OF MIND TELL OTHERS?

"People may hear your words, but
they feel your attitude."
John Maxwell

T his chapter is dedicated to understanding the subtle yet profound messages we convey through our job-seeking attitudes. It illuminates the path to maintaining a hopeful and confident demeanor, which not only shapes our career journey but also influences how potential employers perceive us.

In the realm of job hunting, desperation is a cloak that masks our true potential. Like a shadow, it can follow us into interview rooms and meetings with others and can cast doubt on our abilities. But I've learned, through the wisdom of my faith in God, that we must anchor our state of mind in hope, not in the urgency of our needs.

Let me share a personal revelation I discovered during a particularly trying time in my professional path. I found solace in Proverbs 14:29–30 (NIV), which taught me the virtue of patience and calm. It became clear job seeking is a process where our mental state speaks volumes before we even utter a word. *A peaceful heart does not only lead to a healthy body but also to a promising career.* When we experience peace and trust God for what's to come, we can avoid rushing and taking the first offer we receive. It might be a great offer, but is it the best one?

Building self-confidence is about embracing your worth, knowing you are a child of God, defined not by your employment status but by your divine relationship. *Staying positive isn't just about keeping your spirits high; it's about maintaining a demeanor that attracts opportunities and resonates with those around you.* Remember, God often works through others, so be prepared for new relationships disguised as great opportunities. We should see networking as an extension of fellowship, also known as time spent with a community of friends, a chance to give and receive support in our shared professional quests.

PRACTICAL TIPS AND STRATEGIES

1. Ensure your resume speaks to both your achievements and character. It should be a mirror, reflecting your professional journey and personal growth.
2. Approach each interview as a conversation, not a test

3. Prepare to share, learn, and engage in a dialogue that reveals your strengths and aligns with the company's mission.

4. After an interview, maintain a posture of gratitude and patience. Trust in God's timing and plan for your career. Prayer is the bridge between panic and peace. It's not about reciting perfect words but about honest communication with God, seeking his guidance to align our professional pursuits with his plans.

CALL-TO-ACTION

Reflect on this. Does your job seeker's state of mind showcase a person who trusts in God's plan? Do your interactions with others demonstrate the fruits of the Spirit, patience, kindness, and self-control? Let these questions guide your actions. Today, practice presenting yourself with the confidence of someone who knows their worth in Christ. Let your job search be a testament to your faith as much as your skills. You are not defined by the job you have or how well you do it. You are defined by your relationship with God. King Solomon, in the book of Proverbs, reminds us to use wisdom in our words and actions.

"Whoever is patient has great understanding, but one who is quick-tempered displays folly. A heart at peace gives life to the body, but envy rots the bones."
Proverbs 14:29–30 (NIV)

CLOSING PRAYER

Lord, grant us the serenity to present ourselves with confidence and humility, trusting in your perfect plan for our careers. May our job-seeking journey reflect the steadfast spirit you cultivate within us.

MY TAKE AWAYS

3

THE HEART'S ECHO: LIVING IN A STATE OF GRATITUDE

Sometimes, I find that my heart needs
training more than my brain.

invite you on a reflective journey toward cultivating a state of gratitude. It's an exploration of how a thankful heart can transform our perspective, especially during the uncertainties of job seeking. By adopting a stance of gratitude, we align ourselves more closely with God's intentions, opening pathways to joy and peace.

"If only I had... I just need more.... I would finally be happy if...."

In pursuing a career and success, it's easy to be ensnared by a mindset of scarcity—fixating on what we lack rather than what we possess. I remember articulating countless "if only" statements, believing satisfaction was just one achievement away. However, I've learned that such thoughts are fleeting and do not contribute to a lasting state of contentment. We usually don't find long-term satisfaction by getting more of anything because we eventually want more again. Happiness, which is temporary, comes from external happenings. *True joy comes from within.* Gratitude is the cornerstone of a joyful life, a sentiment echoed in Philippians 4:6–7 (NIV). It's about appreciating our blessings, from the mundane—like running water—to the profound—the ultimate sacrifice of God. Gratitude reorients our hearts toward God's abundance, steering us away from the pitfalls of a perpetual need for happiness.

Understand fulfillment doesn't stem from accumulating more but from appreciating what's already given. Learn to cultivate thankfulness not as a fleeting emotion but as a disciplined approach to life. Discover how expressing gratitude can enhance relationships and open doors to new opportunities and blessings. *"Sometimes I find my heart needs training more than my brain."*

PRACTICAL TIPS AND STRATEGIES

1. Trust in the Lord: Strengthen your faith by entrusting your desires and job search to God, and practice gratitude for his unwavering presence.
2. Engage with Scripture: Find solace and guidance in daily devotionals and Scripture, allowing God's Word to nurture a grateful spirit.

3. Serve Passionately: Volunteer in areas that ignite your passion, using your God-given talents to serve others and, in turn, nurture a grateful heart.

4. Consider how living in gratitude changes your perspective on the job search. Does it alleviate anxiety? Does it enhance your interactions? Reflect on the ways gratitude shifts your focus from what you lack to the abundance God provides.

CALL-TO-ACTION

Today, take a moment to write down three things you're grateful for. Share your gratitude with others and notice the shift in your spirit as you do.

> *"Every good and perfect gift is from above, coming down from the Father of the heavenly lights, who does not change like shifting shadows."*
> James 1:17 (NIV)

CLOSING PRAYER

Dear heavenly Father, in our quest for fulfillment, help us find true contentment in your grace. May our hearts be filled with gratitude for all the blessings, seen and unseen, as we trust in your loving provision.

MY TAKE AWAYS

_____

_____

_____

_____

_____

_____

_____

_____

_____

_____

_____

_____

HOPE: TRUSTING THE PLAN FOR YOUR CAREER

God didn't make it happen to me.
He let it happen for me.

H ave you ever considered exploring the very essence of hope and its undeniable reality in job searching and personal tribulations? It's a testimony to the idea that even when all seems lost, hope remains a steadfast companion, illuminating the path God set for each of us.

Life's darkest moments often bring into question our self-worth and purpose. I remember a year that tested my faith and resolve: 2008. It was a year of profound loss—my father, William, my fiancé, and my longstanding twenty-three-year career in educational leadership, all within five months. Then, within the next three years, I lost my brother and my mom, too. The grief was all-consuming, and in its wake, I found myself devoid of hope and isolated from the world. Needless to say, I was depressed. Do you know what it feels like to sit in isolation, not caring how you look or smell, not bathing for weeks at a time, and just being content with feeling useless? Well, my darkest days were still ahead. What was wrong? I believed my life was worthless because I could not find a job. I clearly defined my life by my title, my career, and my position of authority. As many of you may know from your personal experiences, when grieving, you focus all your thoughts and energy on your career. If you may remember, I had no career.

Yet, it was during this period of profound despair that hope showed its resilient face. The turning point came unexpectedly, through a television commercial in the wee hours of the morning inviting me to a church. In noting the location, I blamed the "holy rollers" of that church for the traffic that always seemed to bottleneck the parkway at that exit. Then, months later, I received a direct-mailing postcard that found its way to me as if by divine intervention. I felt a moment of fear that God actually knew where I lived. Ignoring these signs initially, I nearly succumbed to despair and planned suicide by swallowing several bottles of Valium. But I heard an inaudible voice—the Holy Spirit—that halted my attempt. It spoke and reminded me of my worth and the joy I felt at serving others for many years through volunteering. I questioned the origin of the inaudible voice. However, I was puzzled and remember arguing with the voice and questioning the right this male voice had saying what he was saying. I wanted to hope. But it was so hard to give it another chance.

My obedience to the Holy Spirit led me to gather all the pills, toss them out, and look for ways to volunteer and help others. Volunteering actually opened the door to my next job as a CEO for a non-profit. Prior to this job offer, I was volunteering at two organizations so that I could remain active and bring value wherever I volunteered. Through my volunteer service, my abilities were recognized by these non-profits that began to consider the results I was bringing through the training and mentorship that I offered. Within a few months of volunteering, I was invited to meetings where I could further share my passion. This led me to a CEO position at a non-profit.

One day at work at this non-profit, I received a call asking if I would like to receive some backpacks filled with school supplies for the children in my non-profit. I accepted, and we exchanged emails for the logistics of picking up three hundred backpacks. On that day, after hyperventilating because of the impossible coincidence, I discovered it was that very same church on that street whose commercial I had seen on television that one night while sitting in isolation, stinking, and plotting the end of my life. It was not a coincidence; God was redirecting me. It was an affirming experience that not only restored my faith in my professional capabilities but also started my quest to discover my spiritual life by first becoming curious. How about you? Are you bold enough to be curious? *Are you willing to believe at least for a minute so you can take that bold step and wonder if there is a God who can bring you hope the way he did for me? Looking back, I know God didn't make it happen TO me. He let it happen FOR me.*

PRACTICAL TIPS AND STRATEGIES

1. Consider how hope has played a role in your life, especially in times of hardship. Has there been a moment when you felt a divine nudge steering you toward a better path?

2. Encourage others to seek God's direction in times of uncertainty.

3. Think about volunteering to stay engaged, use talents, and potentially open career doors.

4. Consider how the role of service in finding your calling may lead to unexpected opportunities it can bring.

CALL-TO-ACTION

Reflect on how personal crises in your life may have redirected you toward your God-given purpose. How has he done this without you realizing it at the time? Trust how listening to the divine whisper can lead to transformation and new beginnings for you. What are areas of your life where hope seems dim? Invite God into those spaces. Consider volunteering as a step toward discovering his plan for you.

Another recent career change led me to this point today as I write these chapters for you. I am a changed person because of God. I no longer define my life based on the career I have chosen, whether I have a job or no job. My life is defined by my life with Christ. Don't give up hope. God knows where you are with your endless search for that job you are hoping for. I know it seems like it will never happen. I know sometimes you feel worthless and depressed. Connect with God. Take a chance and give him your heart. He will do wonders. I didn't know God had a plan for my life. He has one for you, too.

> *"For I know the plans I have for you," declares the LORD, "plans to prosper you and not to harm you, plans to give you hope and a future."*
> Jeremiah 29:11 (NIV)

CLOSING PRAYER

Lord, in the quiet despair of our job searches and personal trials, we ask you to be our beacon of hope. Help us hear your voice, see your hand at work in our lives, and follow the path you have laid out for us with trust and gratitude.

MY TAKE AWAYS

LET'S GET STARTED!

THROUGH THICK AND THIN: THE BUDDY SYSTEM

"To add value to others, one must first value others."
John Maxwell

The voyage of job-seeking is an expedition often best navigated with a companion. This chapter explores the dynamic advantages of partnering with a fellow job seeker, transforming the quest from a solitary struggle into a shared adventure of growth and mutual success.

In the potential chaos of career transition, the presence of a like-minded ally can turn the tide of the journey. A buddy system in job searching is akin to having a mirror that reflects not only your strengths but also the areas where you need to grow. It's the candid voice that offers constructive feedback, the sounding board for rehearsing interviews, and the shared toolbox for fresh perspectives and ideas.

Is something stopping you from working with someone else? Don't you want someone to help you, guide you, and give you honest feedback? *Perhaps it is your own heart in the way of asking or accepting help from someone.* Are you refusing to ask for help because you might have to admit you need help after all? Often, it's the truth we deny. Why? If you're having trouble letting go of any potential pride that will get in your way, you're only deceiving yourself. OUCH! You might know what you need to know. However, someone also might have a better idea, perspective, or critique that can help you improve what you know. Perhaps you and your buddy can help each other with your work experience statements and how to create them when you get stuck. I have included **QR Codes** in this chapter so you can scan and download two worksheets that will help you with this task.

PRACTICAL TIPS AND STRATEGIES

1. Collaborate with your buddy on resume reviews and mock interviews.
2. Share job leads and networking opportunities.
3. Hold each other accountable for application goals and personal development.
4. Celebrate each other's progress and support through setbacks.

HOW A BUDDY CAN HELP YOU

1. A buddy will be honest with you about your resume and interview skills.
2. A buddy can share their perspective of how you sound to an employer during a mock interview.
3. A buddy can help you reword things when you are stuck because you might be too stubborn to think differently or admit someone else knows a better way to phrase something.
4. A buddy is much needed to practice with so you can help each other with mock interviews.
5. You share the same thoughts and struggles with another job seeker.
6. You can help each other identify potential job opportunities.
7. You can network with each other.

CALL-TO-ACTION

Reflect on the value of having a companion in your job search. How can a buddy enhance your journey? Are you open to giving and receiving honest feedback? Reach out to a fellow job seeker. Initiate a partnership where you can both benefit from mutual support. Set a plan for how you'll assist each other and commit to regular check-ins.

You are not alone on this journey. King Solomon was very wise. Life is not just about helping others when they need help. It's about having a servant's heart that wants to bless others just because God loves us, too. Our gratitude to the Lord is so great that it is our natural desire to build loving relationships with others so we can shine and let them know the love of Jesus that beams in us. Let God's love shine through as you buddy up with someone.

> *"As iron sharpens iron, so one person sharpens another."*
> Proverbs 27:17 (NIV)

CLOSING PRAYER

Lord, guide us to those who can walk alongside us on our career journeys. Bless our partnerships so that they may be fruitful and reflect your wisdom and companionship.

PRACTICING YOUR EXPERIENCE STATEMENTS

SKILLS ASSESSMENT WORKSHEET

MY TAKE AWAYS

6

YA GOTTA DO YOUR HOMEWORK

"A lot of hard work is hidden behind nice things."
Ralph Lauren

ntering an interview without thorough preparation is like navigating uncharted waters without a map. This chapter is dedicated to equipping job seekers with strategies for in-depth research and preparation that will set the stage for a successful interview.

Thorough preparation is the foundation upon which successful interviews are built. It involves a deep dive into the company's history, culture, products, and the industry landscape. When you thoroughly research a company, you are effectively aligning yourself with their narrative, demonstrating not just an interest in a position but a commitment to becoming a part of their story and culture.

HERE'S A HOMEWORK CHECKLIST

1. What is the company's mission/vision?
2. What value do you bring to the firm that will stand out?
3. What ideas have you thought of that will improve an existing process as learned through your research?
4. How has your previous experience brought new thinking to something the firm is dealing with?
5. Based on your research, are you aware of funding sources the firm may not presently be accessing?
6. Do you have ideas to offer the firm that may improve unity and engagement that are not mentioned in your research?

Consider the process similar to crafting a tailored suit. Each piece of information you gather is a thread that, when woven together with care, creates a garment that fits the company's specific contours. It's about understanding their challenges and achievements, the competitive landscape they operate within, and the culture they foster. With this knowledge, you can articulate how your unique skills and experiences will not just fit but enhance their tapestry.

Reflecting on my coaching experiences, I remember guiding a job seeker who transformed her prospects with meticulous research. She immersed herself in the company's annual reports, dissected its strategic plans, and even engaged with its content on industry forums. During her interview, she articulated how her skills could be leveraged to advance their new initiatives, citing specific examples from her research. Her preparation demonstrated a profound understanding of the company's direction and her potential role within it.

In preparation, it's also critical to analyze the job description and align it with your skills and experiences. *Tailor your success stories to resonate with the responsibilities and qualifications outlined.* This alignment shows the interviewer you're not just looking for any job, but you are the puzzle piece they've been searching for. As you do this, try using some skills and words from the website to include in your resume as you build your website and prepare for an interview. I have included a **QR code** for you to scan and get a free template to download with a huge collection of descriptors.

PRACTICAL TIPS AND STRATEGIES

1. Conduct a SWOT analysis (Strengths, Weaknesses, Opportunities, Threats) on the company to understand its market position.
2. Analyze the job description meticulously, identifying key skills and experiences you possess that match.
3. Engage with current and former employees, if possible, to gain insider insights into the company culture and expectations.
4. Prepare questions that not only demonstrate your knowledge of the company but also show your eagerness to contribute and learn.
5. Seek to understand where you fit within a company's mission and how you can drive its vision forward. Reflect on your findings and consider how they

resonate with your professional ethos and how they will shape your dialogue in the interview room.

CALL-TO-ACTION

Set aside dedicated time each day leading up to your interview for this research. Create a detailed report for yourself on the company and rehearse how you will incorporate this information into your interview answers.

The book of Proverbs gives us the gift of wisdom. It's sort of a guidebook on how to live your life using wisdom and knowledge in alignment with all things.

"Do your planning and prepare your fields before building your house."
Proverbs 24:27 (NLT)

CLOSING PRAYER

Lord, as we prepare for the opportunities ahead, bestow upon us the wisdom to understand, the diligence to seek knowledge, and the clarity to share our vision. May our preparations be thorough, our intentions pure, and our actions aligned with your will.

HELPFUL DESCRIPTORS FOR RESUME BUILDING

MY TAKE AWAYS

_____

_____

_____

_____

_____

_____

_____

_____

_____

_____

_____

_____

_____

_____

7

SHOWCASING YOUR VALUE: CRAFTING A RESULTS-DRIVEN RESUME

Don't give up! If he started it, trust him to finish it.

T he journey toward a career that not only fulfills our professional aspirations but also aligns with our values begins with a single yet significant step: the resume. Here, we dig deep into the art and science of creating a resume that speaks not just of tasks completed but, more importantly, the value delivered and the impact made. Let me re-emphasize it's not about what you did; it's about what you achieved. It's output vs. outcome. You may experience a learning curve when repositioning your thinking. *"Don't give up! If he started it, trust him to finish it."*

In my years as a career coach, the one document that stands as a testament to a professional's journey is the resume.

It's a reflection of not only what you've done but how well you've done it. Consider the resume as a canvas where your career stories are painted not in broad, undefined strokes but with precise, impactful touches that highlight the results of your labor.

For instance, consider the task of auditing customer billing—a role that may seem mundane. Yet, when you frame it as an action that unveiled a significant financial oversight, leading to the recovery of substantial receivables, you transform a simple task into a narrative of accomplishment. It's about bringing to life the outcomes of your efforts, breathing vibrancy into what might otherwise be a monochromatic list of duties. This section has a **QR code** that will lead you to free cheat sheets to help you with many strategic tips on improving your resume.

I recall the time I assisted a young professional, eager but inexperienced, in reshaping his resume. He had the common "duties performed" list, which, while accurate, failed to capture the essence of his contributions. We sat down and sifted through each role, asking, "What changed because of what you did?" The answers were enlightening. Not only did we discover his work had directly led to increased efficiencies, but we also unearthed stories of innovation and leadership that had been buried beneath the humdrum of daily tasks.

PRACTICAL TIPS AND STRATEGIES

1. Start by reviewing each point on your resume and ask yourself, "What was the tangible outcome of this task?

2. Reframe your statements to highlight these outcomes, using metrics and data where possible.

3. Balance the quantifiable achievements with qualitative results, such as improvements in team dynamics or customer satisfaction. A resume must be a dynamic testament to your professional narrative, highlighting the measurable impact of your contributions.

4. Reflect on your career highlights and ask yourself, "How have my actions left a lasting impact on the organizations I have been a part of?" Contemplate how you can continue to create value in your professional endeavors.

CALL-TO-ACTION OR NEXT STEPS

Take a moment today to revisit your resume. Identify at least one experience where you can shift the focus from task to impact and rewrite it to reflect the value you brought to the role.

> *"As Jesus and his disciples were on their way, he came to a village where a woman named Martha opened her home to him. She had a sister called Mary, who sat at the Lord's feet listening to what he said. But Martha was distracted by all the preparations that had to be made. She came to him and asked, "Lord, don't you care that my sister has left me to do the work by myself? Tell her to help me!" "Martha, Martha," the Lord answered, "you are worried and upset about many*

things, but few things are needed—or indeed only one. Mary has chosen what is better, and it will not be taken away from her."
Luke 10:38–42 (NIV)

CLOSING PRAYER

Father, as we seek to present ourselves in the best light in our professional journeys, may we always remember our worth is not defined solely by our achievements but by the integrity and effort we put into them. Let us pray our endeavors may not only bring success in our careers but also glory to God's kingdom and that with your guidance, those who will be reading my resume will see I am a person of character.

RESUME TIPS

MY TAKE AWAYS

_____

_____

_____

_____

_____

_____

_____

_____

_____

_____

_____

_____

HARNESSING HUMILITY: THE CORNERSTONE TO INTERVIEW MASTERY

"True humility is not thinking less of yourself; it's thinking of yourself less."
C.S. Lewis

T he journey toward career fulfillment is often punctuated by pivotal moments—and few are as critical as the job interview. This chapter unpacks the importance of preparation, humility, and trust in both oneself and God's plan as we navigate the intricate dance of interviews. It's more than showcasing skills; it's about demonstrating wisdom, understanding company culture, and aligning with a mission greater than us.

We often think we are prepared for an interview because we believe we know how to do the job because we possess all the skills. Being prepared includes much more than knowing the skills needed. You first must know how to convey to the employer that you are knowledgeable. *There's a huge difference between being a brilliant mathematician and having the skills and capacity to teach mathematics.*

In my years of guiding others as a career coach, I've seen many approach interviews with a mixture of excitement and dread. They often believe having the necessary skills is sufficient. Yet, the art of the interview lies in conveying not just what you know but who you are—and this is where the wisdom and discernment we pray for come into play. *It's about aligning your heart with your head, letting humility lead your responses, and recognizing the interview as a two-way street.*

PRACTICAL TIPS AND STRATEGIES

1. Research the company thoroughly, going beyond the "what" to understand the "why" behind its mission and values.
2. Be adaptable, showing willingness to integrate your skills with the company's unique methods.
3. Prepare questions that showcase your insight into the company's challenges and culture.
4. Approach the interview as a conversation, not an interrogation.
5. Reflect on your interview preparation as a mirror to your character. Do you approach it with the humility that leaves room for God's guidance? How does your preparation align with your faith and professional

goals? Take a moment to consider how you can integrate humility and wisdom into your next interview strategy.

Always remember to pray before your interview and be grateful after each interview, no matter how you feel it went. **Lean in on God and trust he is doing what he needs to do unseen.** Your faith will help you ease your anxiety.

CALL-TO-ACTION

Have you researched the people who potentially might be at the interview? Can you identify any online videos of these people so you can get familiar with their speaking style, their mannerisms, and any personal info that might be revealed such as a hobby or personal viewpoint?

Before your next interview, spend time in quiet reflection or prayer, seeking clarity and peace. Use the tools available, like the resources on my website, to craft responses that resonate with authenticity and humility. Remember to prepare yourself to have a humble heart. Trust God. You can use many free books on my website to prepare for a great interview experience. Take advantage of them.

"Humble yourselves, therefore, under God's mighty hand, that he may lift you up in due time. Cast all your anxiety on him because he cares for you."
1 Peter 5:6–7 (NIV)

CLOSING PRAYER

Dear Lord, grant us the serenity to enter interviews with hearts grounded in your peace. Let us remember that while we prepare extensively, it is your will that ultimately places us where we are meant to be.

MY TAKE AWAYS

_____

_____

_____

_____

_____

_____

_____

_____

_____

_____

_____

_____

_____

IN THE
THICK
OF IT

SEEING FROM THE EMPLOYER'S PERSPECTIVE

Think! What do they want to hear from me?

f you read any chapter in this handbook—**THIS IS THE MUST**! Imagine you're finally being interviewed, excited to give it your best shot. You've been preparing and rehearsing. The employer asks you a pretty simple question. So, without truly understanding what the employer is asking because you're trying to fit your ideas into his question, you "vomit" a sea of thoughts, and the employer interrupts you. Some might see this as passion. However, if you did not think through the question and listen carefully before you respond, you would realize that's not what the employer wanted to hear; rather, that's what you wanted to say.

One of the most valuable pieces of wisdom I can ever share with you is to think like an employer. This chapter explores the pivotal shift from a job seeker's viewpoint to an employer's mindset. *Understanding an employer's needs, vision, and the value they seek in a candidate is more than a strategy; it's a pathway to meaningful employment.* This chapter will guide you through this transformative way of thinking, ensuring you stand out as a candidate who doesn't just seek a position but who brings intrinsic value to the role.

Embarking on the job search journey, I've often witnessed clients struggling to connect their skills and experiences with the needs of potential employers. This disconnect is reminiscent of my early days in career coaching, where I, too, focused on showcasing credentials over understanding the employer's mission. Like a lighthouse seeking to guide ships to shore, I realized one must illuminate the path not just by shining light but also by understanding the sea's unpredictable nature.

Crafting your resume or preparing for an interview is not about pouring out every achievement or skill you possess; it's about aligning your contributions with the employer's goals. Consider the job description as a map where X marks the spot of the employer's needs. Your task is to draw a clear line from your abilities to that X, showing how you can navigate the treacherous waters and bring the ship—your career—to the treasure of success and fulfillment.

Remember the biblical narrative of Jesus sending out his disciples (Matthew 10:16)? He instructed them to be "shrewd as snakes and as innocent as doves." This wisdom transcends time and applies to our professional endeavors. Being shrewd in this context means being astute and keenly aware of the employer's perspective, while innocence lies in the purity of your intentions to serve and contribute to the organization's mission.

So, in all you do to identify a great leader at a new job to work with, be shrewd with your questions and responses. Think from the employer's perspective. Share the wisdom and knowledge they would like to hear that would help them choose you as the only candidate right for the position.

PRACTICAL TIPS AND STRATEGIES

1. Study the job description and tailor your resume to address specific points mentioned.
2. During interviews, focus on how your skills can solve problems the employer faces.
3. Network with intention, seeking to understand industry needs and how you can meet them.
4. Prepare stories that illustrate how you've previously aligned with an employer's mission.
5. Reflect on your experiences: how have they prepared you to meet an employer's needs?
6. Contemplate on times when you've adapted your skills to serve a greater mission.
7. Pray for the insight to see beyond the job description and understand the heart of the organization you wish to join.

CALL-TO-ACTION

Today, take a moment to reevaluate your resume or your approach to interviews. Are you clearly demonstrating how you can meet an employer's needs? Make it your next step to realign your professional narrative with this perspective.

> *"I am sending you out like sheep among wolves. Therefore, be as shrewd as snakes and as innocent as doves."*
> Matthew 10:16 (NIV)

CLOSING PRAYER

Heavenly Father, grant us the wisdom to see our careers through your eyes and the eyes of those we seek to serve in the workplace. May we approach our job search with the shrewdness and innocence you taught, aligning our abilities with the needs of others, serving not just with our hands but with hearts aligned with your purpose.

MY TAKE AWAYS

_____

_____

_____

_____

_____

_____

_____

_____

_____

_____

_____

_____

_____

CHARTING THE
INTERVIEW JOURNEY

*"God never said that the journey will be easy, but
he did say that the arrival will be worthwhile."*
Max Lucado

T he interview process can be a tumultuous sea of emotions and expectations, both for the job seeker and the employer. This chapter delves into the reality of interviews, the preparation required, and the grace we must afford others and ourselves in this crucial phase of career development.

I've often likened the interview process to navigating uncharted waters. Each interview is a unique voyage, and it's not uncommon to encounter rough seas in the form of nervous employers or unexpected questions. I recall a client who once entered what seemed like a disorganized interview with the employer late and ill-prepared. Rather than seeing this as a red flag, my client took the helm and guided the conversation with poise and led with his own questions, actually helping the employer to be more comfortable. It was a testament to his preparedness and adaptability—indispensable traits in any professional setting.

On this journey, it's essential to maintain an attitude of grace. Employers, like candidates, are fallible. They, too, can be swept up in the stress of finding the right fit for their team. *Remember, an interview is a shared experience, and while it's important to present oneself authentically, it's equally vital to extend understanding to those on the other side of the table.* This understanding stems from our faith, which teaches us to be patient and kind, for our paths are often directed by hands unseen.

When you step into an interview, you're not just being assessed on your skills and experience—you're also being evaluated on your fit within a team and an organization. This is why engaging with the process as a dialogue, not a test, is crucial. Express your work ethic, your passion, and your vision, but also be an active listener, picking up on cues about company culture and values.

I know we often tend to get extra nervous on the day of an interview. That morning, we might find ourselves flipping through all kinds of papers, looking at multiple pages covered in sticky notes. To help you prepare calmly, I have created a cheat sheet for you to fill in all the salient points you would want to remember. Scan the **QR code** in this chapter to download this great tool. I think you'll find it very helpful.

WHAT YOU MIGHT EXPERIENCE DURING AN INITIAL INTERVIEW

1. You might be interviewed by an employee who serves as the company filter. It also might be an HR team member, or it might even be your direct report. This generally depends on the size of the company.
2. A chance to share your work experience and specific skills.
3. You'll be given opportunities to highlight some of your more outstanding accomplishments.
4. You will absolutely hear about the company's vision and mission.
5. They will share about the role and how it impacts the overall mission.
6. Potentially, a timeline of projects will be shared, as well as what your involvement might look like.
7. You might interact with employees in the same department.
8. You'll have an opportunity to ask key questions at the end of the interview.
9. You'll be expected to respond to several behavioral questions that will give the employer insight into how you think, act, and respond to workplace situations.

WHAT YOU MIGHT EXPERIENCE DURING A FOLLOW-UP INTERVIEW

1. Questions at this level usually include more content about the actual work you would do and how aligned your skills are with the demands of this position.

2. More information will be shared about the internal operations and culture of the company.
3. You will possibly learn about growth opportunities.
4. Depending on their assessment of you, more information may be divulged about a benefits package.
5. Opportunities to meet staff and engage each other with work-related questions might happen.

PRACTICAL TIPS AND STRATEGIES

1. Embrace each interview as an opportunity to demonstrate flexibility and leadership.
2. Prepare for varying interview formats and expectations at different stages.
3. Use grace as a guiding principle, reflecting a Christ-like demeanor even in challenging circumstances.
4. Consider how you can use the interview process as a mirror—one that not only reflects your qualifications but also your character. Are you as prepared to show understanding and compassion as you are to discuss your achievements? How does this align with the values we hold dear in our faith?

CALL-TO-ACTION

Take time to prepare for the unexpected in interviews. Practice grace and humility, and remember that every interview, regardless of its outcome, is a step forward in God's plan for you.

God encourages us through his Word and his worship,

and he uses each of us to encourage each other through our love for him. He is more than sufficient. Do not be afraid, he reminds us, because he will give us the strength to overcome our troubles when we look to him. Lean on Jesus and not our own understanding of how to solve our problems or have our prayers answered. We can do nothing to earn God's love as he already loves us as his children.

> *"So do not fear, for I am with you; do not be dismayed, for I am your God. I will strengthen you and help you; I will uphold you with my righteous right hand."*
> Isaiah 41:10 (NIV)

CLOSING PRAYER

Lord, as we navigate the interviews ahead, fill us with your wisdom and peace. Help us be gracious in our judgment and steadfast in our faith, knowing you are with us in every word we speak and every step we take.

PRE-INTERVIEW WORSKSHEET

MY TAKE AWAYS

_____

_____

_____

_____

_____

_____

_____

_____

_____

_____

_____

_____

_____

THE FAMOUS FIRST AND
SCARIEST QUESTION

"Thinking will not overcome fear, but action will."
W. Clement Stone

T he voyage into the heart of an interview often begins
with the daunting question, "Tell me a little about
yourself." This prompt, while seemingly simple, can
unsettle even the most seasoned professionals. Here, we
will guide you through crafting a response that showcases your wisdom, aligns with the employer's mission,
and highlights how your experiences are a perfect fit for
the role you desire.

In my coaching experience, I've witnessed countless individuals confront the open-ended nature of this question.
It's the first hurdle in an interview and sets the tone for what
follows. *The key isn't just to survive this moment but to thrive*

within it. When asked to share about yourself, this is an unparalleled opportunity to connect your experiential narrative to the company's vision.

Too often, I have heard clients begin with their birthplace, which continues into a biography that includes everything they've done, and finally, ten minutes later, he's arrived at his first job. This is what I affectionately call "vomiting." You'll hear my new meanings as you peruse through this handbook. At this point, I would not be surprised if you had to wake the employer from a brief nap. Obviously, we don't want to tread into this territory.

I would like to share a handful of the responses I have received during some of the hundreds of interviews I have conducted. Here is how some responses began:

- "Well, I was born in…"
- "I'm not sure where to begin."
- "Do you really just want to know a little bit? I have a lot to tell you."
- "Ummm…hmmmmm"
- "So, I love your company. I follow everything you do all the time."
- "How far back should I go?"

I advise clients to anchor their answers in their professional journey, focusing on moments and decisions shaped by their skills and passion. For instance, an analyst seeking a role at a hospital could start by sharing a childhood anecdote about a love for numbers, then bridge to their recent experiences in finance, and finally express their commitment to patient care, mirroring the hospital's ethos of compassion.

THREE BASIC STEPS TO ANSWER THIS QUESTION

1. Express your passion for this industry infused into your experience and wisdom.
2. Align it to the company's mission.
3. Add how your previous skills and experience will help them deliver the mission of this present company in a new and creative format and set them up for growth.

This approach transforms a potentially paralyzing question into a powerful platform to convey your enthusiasm and passion for the role, your understanding of the company, and your readiness to contribute meaningfully to their mission.

PRACTICAL TIPS AND STRATEGIES

1. Before the interview, reflect deeply on your career journey and identify experiences that showcase your skills and passion.
2. Research the company's mission thoroughly and think about how your experience complements its objectives.
3. Craft a narrative that connects your past achievements with the potential contributions you can make to the company.

4. Practice delivering your response with confidence and clarity, ensuring it feels natural and authentic.

5. As you reflect on the "tell me about yourself" question, consider how your response aligns with the company's mission. Ask yourself if you're clearly communicating not just your qualifications but your eagerness and capacity to fulfill the role. Use this question as a moment to underscore your unique value and how it resonates with the employer's vision.

CALL-TO-ACTION

1. Develop a tailored response to the "Tell me about yourself" question for your next interview.

2. Rehearse it until it feels second nature, and remember, this is your moment to shine.

3. Remember that employers are familiar with your capability and experience based on your resume. Use this as an opportunity to meld your passion for the position with the mission.

Apostle Paul, imprisoned in Rome, facing eventual death, sends his final letter to Timothy, whom he had entrusted to carry on the work he began. He loves Timothy like a son and greatly wants to share with him the wisdom that comes from his belief in Christ and the mission he was selected to carry out. He advises Timothy to make good choices, deny false teachings, and be faithful and also reminds him any fear he has does not emanate from God.

"For the Spirit God gave us does not make us timid, but gives us power, love and self-discipline."
2 Timothy 1:7 (NIV)

CLOSING PRAYER

Lord, grant us the wisdom to see our past experiences as stepping stones to future opportunities. Help us confidently articulate our stories and align our professional paths with your divine guidance.

MY TAKE AWAYS

_____

_____

_____

_____

_____

_____

_____

_____

_____

_____

_____

_____

12

STRATEGIC STORYTELLING: MASTERING THE P-A-R-T TECHNIQUE

"Be interesting, be enthusiastic...
and don't talk too much."
Norman Vincent Peale

When navigating the landscape of job interviews, understanding how to articulate your experiences in a compelling way is crucial. Here, I unveil the PART (Problem-Action-Result-Twist) statement, a powerful framework for constructing narratives that resonate with employers and demonstrate your capacity for reflection and growth.

Don't you love it when a great storyteller keeps you mesmerized? You are captivated until the end of the story. It's a talent you can adapt and use to your benefit during interviews.

After all, the best interview experiences are the ones that feel like they were simply great conversations. Every interview is an opportunity to narrate your professional journey in a way that showcases your potential through storytelling, too. The PART statement is a technique I often reflect upon in my coaching, guiding many through the nuances of behavioral questions. This approach is about painting a vivid picture of your problem-solving abilities and how your actions lead to tangible results, but also about the twist—the invaluable lessons learned.

For example, when faced with a query about a failure or a challenging situation, the PART framework helps you pivot from simply recounting events where you faced a challenge with potentially poor results to revealing insights and lessons learned. It's akin to sharing a parable; the story isn't just about the events that occurred but about the morals and wisdom gleaned.

Here is an example of a PART Statement about a personal experience of my own:

When asked how I handled a situation that didn't go well because of a decision I made.

I led a particular project that created a massive opportunity for families to visit the museums in NYC for free during the Christmas season. I spent a great deal of time doing research, negotiating, and networking with museum curators for free access for 275K families for one week. I even created a booklet that included scavenger hunts and games to play in a couple of the museums and was translated into eight different languages. I was able to negotiate with many museums, and many families were thrilled at the extensive admission costs they were able to avoid.

However, after reviewing the success of the project with the museums, only about 1 percent of 275K families took advantage of this great opportunity. I discovered some museums were not of interest to the families, and they were more interested in interactive opportunities available. I learned from this that instead of assuming everyone would love to visit art museums, I should have included feedback and sought the opinions of real families to discuss the options. By excluding other's opinions, I missed such a valuable opportunity for families to contribute, participate, and gain wonderful experiences during the holiday season. Inclusion leads to a richer experience.

So, as demonstrated here, I shared about a time when I made a decision as a leader, but since then, I have learned to think more broadly and give ownership to others as well.

This section has a **QR code** that will lead you to free cheat sheets to help you with PART Statements. They will give you the opportunity to be very prepared with this storytelling technique during an interview.

PRACTICAL TIPS AND STRATEGIES

1. Prepare by reflecting on various challenges you've faced and the actions you took.
2. Identify clear results from your actions, quantifiable where possible.

3. Contemplate the lessons learned and be ready to share these "twists" with sincerity.
4. Practice your PART statements and have scenarios ready to share because most interviews include these types of questions. They convey a great deal of what they can expect from you as an employee.

CALL-TO-ACTION

The PART statement is more than just a method for answering interview questions; it's a reflection of a growth mindset. Contemplate the challenges you've faced in your career. How have they shaped you? How have they prepared you for future opportunities?

Review your professional experiences and craft PART statements you can utilize in your next interview. By doing so, you'll be ready to present a narrative that not only outlines your qualifications but also your character and ability to learn from every situation.

The Sermon on the Mount is the most impactful speaking engagement of all time! Jesus encourages us to build our faith and trust on a strong foundation. He warns us to build our houses on solid rock. So, as you continue your job search, build your trust in his Word and have faith that your passion and desires will be fulfilled in time while you continue to seek him.

"Therefore, everyone who hears these words of mine and puts them into practice is like a wise man who built his house on the rock. The rain came down, the streams rose, and the winds blew and beat against that house; yet it did not fall, because it had its foundation on the rock. But everyone who hears these words of mine and does not put them into practice is like a foolish man who built his house on sand. The rain came down, the streams rose, and the winds blew and beat against that house, and it fell with a great crash."
Matthew 7:24–27 (NIV)

CLOSING PRAYER

May we approach each opportunity with a spirit of wisdom, reflecting on our past to illuminate the path forward. As we articulate our experiences, let us remember our strength and resilience are grounded not in our perfection but in our ability to rise and learn from every fall.

PART STATEMENT WORKSHEETS

MY TAKE AWAYS

_____

_____

_____

_____

_____

_____

_____

_____

_____

_____

_____

_____

_____

13

THE TWO-WAY STREET
OF INTERVIEWS

*Sometimes, we just have to give
people the space to be human.*

n this chapter, we explore the pivotal realization that the
interview process is a dual-sided conversation, not merely
a one-sided interrogation. You'll discover how to navigate
interviews with the discernment to evaluate potential employers, aligning with the right organizational values and leadership styles that resonate with your professional and personal
growth.

Imagine walking into an interview room, your palms
slightly moist, your heart racing a tad faster than usual, and
there sits the hiring manager, portfolio in hand, ready to begin
what at times feels like an inquisition. But wait—something
is different about today. Today, you come with a realization

that changes the entire dynamic. *You are not just here to be discovered; you are also here to seek, to discern if this opportunity aligns with your purpose, your values, and the direction God is leading you.*

Let's break this down:

UNDERSTANDING THE EMPLOYER'S VISION AND LEADERSHIP

I recall the time I sat across from a potential employer whose demeanor was as cold as the stark, lifeless room we were in. The first statement offered to me was, "We will write down every word you say, word for word." Well, needless to say, they lost me. Clearly, their vision was not one of growth and inspiration but of rigid expectations and stern authority. It dawned on me then that to truly thrive and serve with my God-given talents, I needed an environment that valued innovation, encouraged growth, and practiced servant leadership, much like the biblical figures who led not by fear but by faith and example.

The main reason an employee leaves a company is usually not because of the work itself. It's usually because of the lack of or poor leadership, followed by salary. Because of the lack of leadership, an employee becomes discouraged, which triggers the questioning of the salary and if it's worth the toxic environment they are tolerating because they love the work or the people they serve.

EVALUATING COMPANY CULTURE AND MANAGEMENT

A company's culture is the ecosystem in which your career will either flourish like the cedars of Lebanon or wither like a vine without water. Seek signs of a culture that resonates with your core values. When coaching clients, I often advise them to delve into the company's community involvement, as it speaks volumes about their values beyond profit margins. Their culture should also reflect a heart for people, mirroring the servant leadership exemplified by Christ.

Job seekers usually accept a position because they are excited about the mission of the firm. They get discouraged and want to leave a firm when they see poor management and a lack of leadership. *A lack of leadership can lead to disunity and a potentially toxic environment.* Examples of a lack of leadership may look like a disengaged supervisor who is transactional and does not get involved with his employees.

DOES YOUR DIRECT REPORT:

1. Meet with you on a consistent scheduled basis?
2. Stop and have impromptu conversations with you when he/she detects a change in your attitude?
3. Make themself available to listen to you?
4. Have honest conversations with you that include true assessments and strategies to improve weaknesses?
5. Help you grow through opportunities that challenge your skills?

6. Own their own actions, especially when they have made poor decisions?

YOUR ROLE IN THE INTERVIEW

When you're in an interview, think of David before Goliath—he didn't stand before the giant to be judged; he stood to show who he was and what he stood for. Your resume and your skills are your stones in the sling. Use the interview to demonstrate not just what you can do but who you are and how you represent the unique creation God has made you to be.

CREATING A TWO-WAY DIALOGUE

Engage in the interview as a conversation. When I found myself being interviewed in a room that felt more like a judgment seat than a meeting place, I shifted the narrative. I asked about their mission, their team dynamics, and their definition of success. It turned the table, allowing me to see their true colors and them to see mine—a professional guided by faith, seeking more than just a job, but a calling.

REFLECTING ON LEADERSHIP STYLES

In the realm of leadership, there's a stark contrast between a manager and a leader. Managers might steer the ship, but leaders inspire the crew to row with vigor and purpose. Like Paul's journey, which was fueled by faith and fellowship, seek leaders who fuel their team with inspiration and guidance rather than mere directives and demands.

PRACTICAL TIPS AND STRATEGIES

1. Compile a list of questions that reflect not only your career goals but also your personal values and beliefs. Always be prepared for the next step at this point. Think about the employer's answers and how they might transform into questions for you. How would you answer?

2. Observe the interviewers' behavior and the office environment; they are indicators of the company culture.

3. Reflect on your experiences and identify what work environments made you thrive or dive, using these insights to guide your evaluation.

4. Ask yourself, did the employer's vision resonate with your values? Did the leadership style encourage a growth mindset reminiscent of the nurturing Christlike leadership we aspire to? Reflect on these aspects through prayer, seeking clarity and guidance from the Holy Spirit.

Do you have discernment? In other words, can you judge well and clearly what is not obvious and straightforward? When you are praying, ask God for the discernment you need to see past what is being shared with you to understand what information your discernment is showing you about the leaders of this company. The Holy Spirit gives us the gift of discernment. While you are participating in your interview, look for signs of exemplary leadership. Are these people the leaders you want to follow and emulate, not just the firm that you want to join? Do you feel they offer you the future that will help you achieve success through their leadership? Don't be carried away by titles and content. Ask questions that will delve into the causes for success in their firm. Just remember that if you are already wondering if it's going to get better working at a firm before you start, consider what it will be like when the honeymoon stage is over.

CALL-TO-ACTION

Today, take a moment to list the qualities you seek in an employer, considering both your career aspirations and your spiritual journey. Prepare questions for your next interview that align with these qualities, setting the stage for a mutually beneficial dialogue.

Solomon asked God for discernment and wisdom when he became king after his father, King David. He had a nation to lead. He was as scared as a little child because he felt he didn't know what he needed to know to discern the difference between right and wrong.

"So give your servant a discerning heart to govern your people and to distinguish between right and wrong. For who is able to govern this great people of yours?"
1 Kings 3:9 (NIV)

CLOSING PRAYER

Heavenly Father, guide us as we navigate the path of our careers. Grant us the wisdom to see beyond the surface in interviews to discern whether an opportunity aligns with your will for us. May we find the place where our professional talents and spiritual gifts can flourish together.

MY TAKE AWAYS

_____

_____

_____

_____

_____

_____

_____

_____

_____

_____

_____

_____

14

INDIVIDUAL AND PANEL INTERVIEWS: A DANCE OF DISCERNMENT

"God speaks in the silence of the heart.
Listening is the beginning of prayer."
Mother Teresa

T he interview process is a delicate interplay of personalities and professional competencies. We will explore the nuances of individual versus panel interviews and how understanding the human aspect of each can significantly influence your performance. Amidst the technical preparation, a grounding in faith can provide the balance you need to navigate these waters. The most overlooked skill needed during interviews...LISTEN.

An interview, be it individual or panel, is more than a

series of questions and answers; it's a window into the emotional and experiential landscape of each participant. As a career coach, I've seen the profound impact that personal challenges can have on an interviewee's performance. It's not uncommon for job seekers to carry the weight of personal issues into an interview room, which can cloud their ability to present their best selves. Here is where our faith steps in, offering a bedrock of peace and wisdom amidst the storm.

Praying for discernment and wisdom can change the atmosphere of an interview from one of fear to one of faith and determination. The dynamic of a one-on-one interview is vastly different from that of a panel interview. Individual interviews often serve as a preliminary filter, while panel interviews introduce the complexity of multiple observers, each bringing their own perspective. In individual settings, it's about connecting with one person and doing your best to engage them in a conversational manner while bearing in mind they are hoping to hear how you will help their firm and not just what you want to share with them.

Panel interviews are about engaging with the collective. Remember, trying to please everyone can be a trap; focus on communicating your truth with clarity and confidence. When participating in a panel interview, make eye-to-eye contact with the whole group. However, when one person asks you a question, answer by focusing on that person first, and as you continue speaking, pan your eyes across the entire panel and then close with your eyes focused back on the person who asked the question. Panel interviews also give existing staff an opportunity to meet you and decide for themselves in their respective roles if you are a good fit for the team. Different perspectives provide further insight and give the existing team a chance to feel the chemistry between you.

The goal of the first one-on-one interview is generally to get to the level two interview. This still might be a one-on-one format, or if the employer is very satisfied with you, it might become a panel interview.

In my experience, I've coached many through these challenges, emphasizing the importance of eye contact, active listening, and strategic communication. I've shared anecdotes, like the one of a student who, in the middle of a panel interview, inadvertently offended a panel member. This taught us all a valuable lesson in handling interruptions with grace. Such instances underscore the need to be as prepared for the interpersonal dance of interviews as for the content.

Just remember, whether it's an individual or a panel interview, you can pray so you will conduct yourself without fear or anxiety. As I always say, pray before and after an interview. Sometimes, insecure people conducting interviews can act with a threatening attitude that invokes fear. This is their leadership style. Most are not like this. Employers want the best from candidates. Strategies for one-on-one interviews differ from those for panel interviews, but the foundation remains the same: know your audience, prepare meticulously, and rely on your faith to guide you through. My heart wants to remind you that God goes before you. So, bring it. I have a **QR code** in this section that will take you to a further list of tips and strategies to use during interviews.

PRACTICAL TIPS AND STRATEGIES

1. In individual interviews, focus on building a rapport with the interviewer.
2. In panel interviews, distribute your attention evenly but anchor your responses to the person who asked the question.
3. Use your body language to engage with each panel member, and when answering a question, conclude by affirming you've addressed the concerns of all.
4. Prepare for both types of interviews with equal diligence, knowing God is with you in both scenarios.
5. Reflect on past interviews and consider moments where you could have shown more grace or discernment. Contemplate how your faith can be a source of strength in future interviews, providing a sense of calm and focus.

CALL-TO-ACTION

Before your next interview, spend time in prayer, asking for the Holy Spirit's guidance. Rehearse not only your answers but also scenarios that might arise during a panel interview. Prepare your heart to be as ready as your mind.

It was time for Moses to announce that Joshua would lead the Israelites into the Promised Land. Moses proclaimed his trust for Joshua in front of all the Israelites to ensure they would respect his authority. With the same faith and trust in God, you will succeed in all God has designed you for, but remember, it will be in his time, not yours. If this job is supposed to be for you, it will be.

> "The LORD himself goes before you and will be with you; he will never leave you nor forsake you. Do not be afraid; do not be discouraged."
> Deuteronomy 31:8 (NIV)

CLOSING PRAYER

Father God, we ask for your presence in every step of our interview process. May we carry the peace that surpasses all understanding into every interview room, be it with an individual or a panel. May your wisdom guide our words and your peace calm our spirits.

JOB INTERVIEW TIPS

MY TAKE AWAYS

_____

_____

_____

_____

_____

_____

_____

_____

_____

_____

_____

_____

_____

15

MASTERING THE DIGITAL HANDSHAKE: SUCCEEDING IN VIRTUAL INTERVIEWS

"It's the little details that are vital. Little things make big things happen."
John Wooden

T he virtual interview has become a mainstay in the modern recruitment process, bridging distances and bringing efficiency into the hiring landscape. This chapter will guide you through the essentials of preparing for a virtual interview, ensuring you can present the best version of yourself, even through a monitor.

The pivot to virtual interviews has been swift, and adapting to this format requires not just technological savvy but a presence of mind and spirit. As with traditional interviews, the foundation of success lies in preparation—both your environment and your soul. In my coaching, I emphasize the importance of preparing for a great virtual interview just as much as an in-person interview.

PRACTICAL POINTERS TO PREPARE FOR A VIRTUAL INTERVIEW

1. Select a private space to reduce interruptions or distractions.
2. Ensure there is very good lighting.
3. Choose a table/desk that will allow you to set up your laptop at a good height for your face to be positioned well in the employer's view.
4. Choose a chair that aligns well with your table/desk height. Please be mindful to avoid chairs that rotate or spin. If you become jittery during the interview, you will start wiggling and moving around in the chair, distracting the employer.
5. Be mindful of what your environment is and what is in view of your camera angle. No need to have laundry hanging on a line behind you.
6. Clear your table/desk space so that you can place any needed documents/notes you want to refer to during the interview.
7. Do a mock interview and set everything up one hour before the interview so that you can avoid technical difficulties when the interview starts.

8. Use sticky notes all around the border of your laptop that contain specific highlights or things you want to absolutely include in your responses.

9. If other family members, friends, or pets are in the space you are using, close the door and put a Do Not Disturb sign on the door, indicating you're being interviewed.

10. Check for clarity and sound on your laptop.

11. Your attire should be appropriate to the culture of the company you are applying to. Please wear a complete outfit, top and bottom. In case you have to get up and get something in the middle of the interview, you want to be fully dressed. You will also feel more prepared if you are dressed properly, even though it's a virtual format.

12. Look at the camera during the interview. We tend to look at the face we see on the screen. In actuality, your face is looking downward if you are not looking at the camera.

13. Ensure your laptop is fully charged or plugged in.

14. Be sure the interview has ended and you have disconnected before you say anything at the end of the interview.

But beyond the physical setup, I've discovered the spiritual preparation to be just as vital. *Prayer before a virtual interview does more than calm nerves—it invites God's presence into your space, guiding your words and demeanor.* It's in these moments of divine connection that the depth of your character can truly shine through the digital interface.

The apostle Paul's exhortation to work enthusiastically for the Lord applies as much to our digital engagements as it does to our physical work and efforts. Approach your virtual interview with the same zeal and dedication as if you were walking into a grand boardroom.

PRACTICAL TIPS AND STRATEGIES

1. Test your technology well in advance to troubleshoot any issues.
2. Use notes strategically, but ensure they don't distract from maintaining eye contact with the camera.
3. Dress fully and professionally to enhance your mindset and readiness.
4. Close all unnecessary applications on your computer to ensure smooth video streaming.
5. Reflect on your readiness for a virtual interview. How does your setup reflect your professionalism? How can prayer and spiritual readiness play a role in your preparation? Review the apostle Paul's teachings—how can you apply his wisdom to remain diligent and hopeful, even in the solitude of a virtual space?

CALL-TO-ACTION

Conduct several mock virtual interviews with a friend or mentor. Assess your technological setup, your interaction with the camera, and how well you communicate your qualifications and passion for the role.

Paul never stopped laboring in his mission to preach the gospel to his brothers and sisters in the church of Rome. He encouraged all to work hard for the Lord but always to do it with zeal. He reminded them to stay true to the Word of God and be devoted to loving one another. So, do what you can always do during this challenging time while you wait for the next step in your career. Be hopeful that regardless of what happens, there is a purpose and a plan for your life.

> *"Never be lacking in zeal, but keep your spiritual fervor, serving the Lord."*
> Romans 12:11 (NIV)

CLOSING PRAYER

Heavenly Father, as we enter the realm of virtual interviews, we ask for your guiding hand over our technology and our hearts. May our screens be a window to our dedication and our spirits.

MY TAKE AWAYS

_____

_____

_____

_____

_____

_____

_____

_____

_____

_____

_____

_____

16

QUESTIONS THAT GET THE EMPLOYER EXCITED

You don't become truly impactful when someone gives you power; you make an impact when you empower others.

The power of inquiry in an interview is not merely a formality; it's an opportunity to showcase genuine interest and gain invaluable insights into the company and your potential role within it. This chapter will guide you through the process of crafting questions that not only reflect your enthusiasm but also reveal the company's vision, culture, and expectations, aligning them with your career trajectory.

What do you mean you don't have any questions? *I suggest you have a minimum of five thought-provoking questions prepared for the end of the interview.* The employer will perceive a lack of questions at the end of the interview to mean you really don't care enough about what the position means and how it impacts the company's overall mission. In my early coaching days, I faced candidates who had solid interviews but faltered at the end because they had either no questions or superficial ones for the employer. I've always emphasized that questions are not just inquiries; they're reflections of your values and vision. The lack of questions can signal disinterest or a lack of preparation, while the right questions can demonstrate foresight and engagement. Check out the full list of sample questions you can consider for your next interview by using the **QR code** in this section.

I recall advising a young professional transitioning from a technical role to a managerial position. Their technical expertise was commendable, but they struggled with the concept of company culture. I encouraged them to ask questions that would uncover the company's values and day-to-day employee experiences. This not only helped them understand the company better but also displayed a thoughtful approach to their potential employer.

The apostle Paul, in his guidance, emphasized wisdom and clarity of purpose. Similarly, when preparing questions for an employer, seek clarity about the role and how it contributes to the company's mission. This clarity will not only help you decide if the company aligns with your career goals but also show the employer you think strategically about your role and its impact.

When crafting questions for different levels of the interview process, categorize them based on the information you need to make an informed decision about the job and demonstrate your strategic thinking to the potential employer.

LEVEL QUESTIONS

- Level 1 questions might delve into the company culture and daily responsibilities.
- Level 2 questions could focus on success metrics and opportunities for growth within the company.
- Level 3 questions might address personal benefits and work-life balance considerations.

POSSIBLE QUESTIONS TO ASK AN EMPLOYER

1. What part of the company culture do you enjoy the most, and what do you find challenging?
2. How do employees work as a team in the dept I am applying to?
3. How will I know I am meeting targets and benchmarks within given timelines?
4. Will I be given honest feedback so I can grow toward surpassing the expectations needed to be considered as a strong team member?
5. What leadership opportunities are made available to the team members, and how are they communicated?
6. What problem keeps the CEO up late at night?
7. Does the firm have a corporate social responsibility program?

8. How would I know if I am being considered for a leadership role?

Bring five questions typed up in priority order. If an employer only allows two, you will know which are the most important questions for you to ask. Have five questions ready, as some of your questions may be answered by the employer during the interview. In this case, where the employer has answered many of your questions while they shared, you don't want to have a blank stare at the end of the interview. Be prepared with five questions, just in case.

PRACTICAL TIPS AND STRATEGIES

1. Research the company thoroughly to tailor your questions to the specific role and the company's strategic goals.
2. Prioritize your questions, keeping the most crucial inquiries ready in case time is limited.
3. Reflect on what you genuinely want to know that wasn't covered during the interview to show you are thinking beyond the role and about the bigger picture.

CALL-TO-ACTION

For your next interview, prepare a set of questions that cover company culture, the role's impact on the company's mission, and personal growth opportunities. Use these questions to engage the interviewer and demonstrate your strategic approach to your career development.

In the book of James, James is speaking to Jewish Christians scattered abroad and reminds them that when you seek God, you must seek him with all your heart.

> *"If any of you lacks wisdom, you should ask God, who gives generously to all without finding fault, and it will be given to you. But when you ask, you must believe and not doubt, because the one who doubts is like a wave of the sea, blown and tossed by the wind. That person should not expect to receive anything from the Lord. Such a person is double-minded and unstable in all they do."*
> James 1:5–8 (NIV)

CLOSING PRAYER:

Dear Lord, grant me the discernment to ask insightful questions that will lead me to your will and align my career with your divine plan. May my inquiries reflect a heart eager to serve and a mind prepared to contribute meaningfully to my workplace.

QUESTIONS THAT GET THE EMPLOYER EXCITED

MY TAKE AWAYS

_____

_____

_____

_____

_____

_____

_____

_____

_____

_____

_____

_____

_____

THE ART OF POST-INTERVIEW GRATITUDE

"At times, our own light goes out and is rekindled by a spark from another person. Each of us has cause to think with deep gratitude of those who have lighted the flames within us."
Albert Schweitzer

O n your career journey, the humble "thank you" holds the power to leave a lasting impression about you. This chapter delves into the nuanced art of gratitude post-interview, transforming a simple gesture into a strategic tool for career advancement.

The post-interview thank you is more than a courtesy; it's a strategic touchpoint. It's a reflection of your character and an echo of your interest in the role. Whether it's through a promptly sent email or a handwritten note, this gesture carries the weight of genuine thankfulness and attention to detail. In my career coaching experience, I've observed that those who approach this step thoughtfully tend to stand out in the memories of their prospective employers.

A thank you email should be sent within twenty-four hours of the interview (not right after the interview), ensuring it conveys sincerity without veering into a request for updates or further interviews. Please try hard to make the thank you email strictly a thank you. When sending this thank you, please do not attach things to it. If you choose to send a card, it signifies a personal touch, a nod to tradition, and a standout move in today's digital world.

Moreover, this chapter encourages you to resist the urge to follow up too soon or too often. Instead, consider sending additional, value-added communications, such as a piece of creative work or letters of recommendation you would like the employer to add to your profile, as a way to remind the employer of your candidacy and interest. *These strategies are like a wink to the employer, serving as informational, "Hi, remember me."*

Reflect on the gratitude you've shown throughout your career search. Does it come from a place of sincerity? Remember, expressing thankfulness is not just about politeness but about embodying the spirit of service and humility central to our faith. Check out the **QR code** to download some free templates you can use in whole or part as a thank-you letter.

PRACTICAL TIPS AND STRATEGIES

1. Send a thank you email within twenty-four hours of the interview.
2. Consider a handwritten thank-you card for a personal touch.
3. Avoid using the "thank you" to ask for updates or to push for the next interview stage.
4. Use subsequent communications to provide additional value rather than to inquire about your application status.
5. Maintain a tone of gratitude, not curiosity or entitlement.

CALL-TO-ACTION

Take the initiative to draft a thank you message you can tailor for each interview. Prepare additional follow-up materials that can be sent judiciously to maintain interest in your application.

When Timothy returned from Corinth, he reported to Apostle Paul that the new believer Christians in Thessalonica were remaining steadfast and strong in their faith, even through the persecution and strife they faced. Regardless of the results of your interview, remain strong and remain grateful.

"Rejoice always, pray continually, give thanks in all circumstances; for this is God's will for you in Christ Jesus."
1 Thessalonians 5:16–18 (NIV)

CLOSING PRAYER

Lord, help us express our gratitude with authenticity and wisdom. May our actions reflect your grace, and may our words of thanks resonate with the sincerity of our hearts. In the spirit of 1 Thessalonians 5:16–18 (NIV), we strive to be joyful, prayerful, and thankful in all circumstances.

HOW DO YOU SAY THANK YOU

MY TAKE AWAYS

18

SO, YOU APPLIED FOR THE SAME JOB TWICE, HUH?

"We make mistakes. But nothing you ever do is beyond the capacity for God to use. You may make mistakes, but God doesn't."
Rick Warren

T he journey of job searching is a test of one's diligence and organizational skills. This chapter will explore the pitfalls of a disorganized job application process, particularly the issues that arise from applying multiple times to the same position, and the strategies to ensure meticulous and intentional job-seeking efforts.

The error of applying more than once to the same job at the same company can be a telltale sign of a disorganized job search approach. It reflects poorly on a candidate, especially when their resume boasts of meticulous attention to detail.

In my career coaching sessions, I've emphasized that the way you search for a job can often reflect how you might perform on the job. For instance, an organized job seeker, who is as systematic and thorough as they claim to be on their resume, would keep track of each application sent, avoiding duplication and ensuring each submission is tailored and intentional.

Consider the job application process as a reflection of your future work habits. Just as a well-organized portfolio suggests proficiency and professionalism, a carefully managed job search indicates a candidate's capacity for structure and detail. Because so many jobs will sound very similar, it's even more important to be organized. An organized job search is a powerful tool in your arsenal. It prevents redundancy, showcases your professionalism, and maintains your reputation in tight-knit professional circles.

To avoid the confusion and embarrassment of multiple applications to the same role, adopt a systematic approach. Create a job search spreadsheet or a dedicated tracking system where you log every position applied for, including dates, the resume version used, and any correspondence received. By investing effort into such a system, you're not only avoiding potential blunders but also positioning yourself as a candidate of choice, someone who exemplifies the organizational skills that are highly valued in any professional setting.

If you scan the **QR code** in this section, it will take you to a system I shared during my classes so you can track everything meticulously and prevent mistakes that might prevent you from getting an offer to interview. Feel free to download the form from my website, marshatom.com.

PRACTICAL TIPS AND STRATEGIES

1. Create a personalized job tracking system using spreadsheets or dedicated software.
2. Maintain meticulous records of applications, follow-ups, and networking contacts.
3. Before submitting an application, double-check your records to ensure it's your first submission to the role.
4. Customize your resume and cover letter for each application to demonstrate your dedication and interest in the specific role.
5. Reflect on your current job search habits. Are they as ordered and methodical as they could be? How can you improve your system to ensure efficiency and effectiveness?

CALL-TO-ACTION

Today, make a commitment to enhance your job search organization. Whether it's by starting a new tracking system or refining an existing one, take the necessary steps to streamline your application process.

Even Paul the apostle was guiding the church of Corinth in his letters, which were filled with instruction. When he heard the church was facing a crisis of unity and ethics, he was encouraging them to understand the importance of doing things in an orderly and organized manner. God loves his church to operate with organization and integrity.

"But everything should be done in a fitting and orderly way."
1 Corinthians 14:40 (NIV)

CLOSING PRAYER

Dear Lord, grant us the wisdom to approach our job search with orderliness and integrity. Help us to be mindful of our methods so that they may reflect the orderly nature of your creation.

SUGGESTED FILING SYSTEM

MY TAKE AWAYS

_____

_____

_____

_____

_____

_____

_____

_____

_____

_____

_____

_____

_____

NOW, WE WAIT AND PRAY

19

THE POWER OF PRAYER IN YOUR CAREER JOURNEY

You are not defined by the job you have; you are defined by the relationship you have with God.

The act of prayer is a profound cornerstone in both personal and professional realms. It offers solace, guidance, and clarity, especially during the trials of job seeking. This chapter explores the multifaceted role of prayer in the job search process, emphasizing its potential to foster wisdom, discernment, and peace of mind.

Prayer is a dialogue with God, a moment to lay bare our deepest desires and fears; it's just between the two of you. No matter your situation or how hopeless you believe it is, God wants to hear from you. In my career, as in life, I've found prayer to be a haven, a place to find solace and seek guidance when making pivotal decisions. In these quiet conversations with God, I have often found clarity and the strength to make choices aligned with his will for my life.

In job searching, prayer becomes an even more critical tool. It's easy to rely solely on our own understanding and rush headlong into decisions we later regret. Prayer slows us down and reminds us to relinquish control and trust in God's plan for our lives. It's a practice in humility, recognizing that while we make plans, God determines our steps. *You are not defined by the job you have; you are defined by the relationship you have with God.*

Why is prayer important during your job-seeking period? Have you ever been so sure of your decision about something you'd bet a million dollars and then discovered you were completely wrong? You know you have. I know I have. Of course, this was followed by, "What was I thinking! How could I have thought that!" Prayer can help you in so many ways. The benefits of prayer are innumerable: it connects us to God, diminishes stress, and provides a platform for self-reflection. *In prayer, we do not find an escape from reality but the courage to face it with a heart fortified by faith.* Whether it's an individual quiet time on a serene beach or communal prayer with friends, the essence remains the same—prayer changes things, often starting with our own hearts.

HERE ARE WAYS PRAYER HAS HELPED ME

1. It slows me down, so I don't make those impetuous decisions I tend to make.
2. It helps me to openly recognize I don't have control of my situation.

3. It reminds me to trust God for what he has in store for my life.
4. It connects me to God and strengthens my relationship with him.
5. It's the reality that I want the result of my prayer to be what God wants for me.
6. It's a way of letting go so that I can get out of God's way so he can do good for me.
7. It helps me be grateful as I pray for things I'm hoping for, and I remember what he has already done for me.

HERE ARE SOME WAYS TO GET COMFORTABLE WITH PRAYER

1. My favorite place to pray is a secluded beach where it feels like it's just the ocean, sand, water, God, and me. I can sit there for hours and just talk to him. Being a resident of the West Coast, this is easy for me to do. I hope you can find a nice, quiet place that you enjoy. It can be in the park, your car, the bathroom, or even in a closet.
2. Use your Bible as a starting point and read some Scriptures that have deep meaning to you. If you don't have any, look for some and write them down, or use some bookmarks or sticky notes in your Bible.
3. Use an audible Bible and listen to the Bible being read to you.

4. Spend some time listening to worship music and listen emphatically to the lyrics and pray while you are worshipping.

5. Pray with friends—you can each take a turn, or all of you can pray at the same time.

PRACTICAL TIPS AND STRATEGIES

1. Find a quiet place where you feel at peace to engage in prayer.

2. Use Scriptures or worship music to guide your prayer if you're unsure where to start.

3. Remember, prayer is personal; it's about your heart's intentions, not the eloquence of words.

4. Incorporate prayer into your daily routine, starting with a few minutes and gradually increasing as you feel led.

5. Contemplate the role prayer plays in your life. How can you integrate this practice more deeply into your career journey? Reflect on times when prayer has provided insight or peace in your decision-making process.

CALL-TO-ACTION

If you haven't already, build a practice of prayer into your job search strategy. Let it be the bedrock upon which you stand as you navigate the complexities of career transitions. I hope prayer becomes part of your daily life. Start slow and pray for a minute two to three times per week. Gradually increase your time and the number of days. I pray you find comfort in prayer, seeking what God has in store for your life.

THIS IS IMPORTANT!

Many people feel church may not be a welcoming place for them. I'm so sorry you might feel this way. I wish there was a way we could just sit and chat for a few minutes. Many believe that to attend church, you've got to have your life in order first. If that were the truth, every church in the world would be completely empty. Churches are filled with broken people like you and ME. This is exactly why we need God. We will never be perfect; we don't seek perfection. We seek love, acceptance, and belonging. If you are still searching for your purpose in life, try praying to God and see where he leads you. However, remember, God is not a vending machine. I used to believe that prayer goes in and out comes your wish. Life doesn't work like that. Trust, faith, patience, and a relationship with God will help you discover your purpose more and more every day.

"Search me, God, and know my heart; test me and know my anxious thoughts. See if there is any offensive way in me, and lead me in the way everlasting."
Psalm 139:23–24 (NIV)

CLOSING PRAYER

Lord, we come before you, seeking your wisdom and peace. As we navigate the uncertainties of job seeking, we ask that you be our guiding light.

MY TAKE AWAYS

_____

_____

_____

_____

_____

_____

_____

_____

_____

_____

_____

_____

20

NAVIGATING THE WAIT WITH GRACE AND STRATEGY

"The power of God will take you out of your
own plans and put you into the plan of God."
Smith Wigglesworth

T he interval between the first interview and the follow-up
can be fraught with uncertainty. This chapter explores
the constructive ways to channel your post-interview
energy and anxieties, transforming the waiting period from a
passive to an active state, aligning with God's timing and will.

After the initial interview, a whirlwind of doubts and
worries can unsettle the most seasoned professionals. These
feelings are natural, but they're also opportunities to reflect,
learn, and prepare for the next steps. *It's in this phase of waiting we can either succumb to negative self-talk or choose to uplift
ourselves through proactive measures and trust in God's plan.*

Negative thoughts may besiege us, questioning our performance or suitability. Yet, as I've learned through my career and helping others, these concerns often say more about our internal state than the reality of the situation. God's guidance during these times is crucial; as we wait on him, we find the strength to wait on the next career move with anticipation, not anxiety.

During this time, it's essential to continue growing, seeking other opportunities, and enriching your professional and personal life. It's a chance to expand your knowledge, network with passion, volunteer, and possibly explore new hobbies or improve existing skills. This proactive approach not only keeps your spirits high but also enhances your professional profile for future opportunities. Remember to enjoy life during this time, too. What fun it is to focus only on the task of a new position and then spend so much time proving yourself in the new position that you forget to carve out time for family, friends, and hobbies.

There's also another part of waiting you may not have thought of. There's a strong chance you have nothing to do with why you haven't heard back yet.

CONSIDER THESE

1. The funding for the position has not been secured yet.
2. The person presently working in that position has not officially left yet.

3. The department you interviewed for might be a new one, and the interview process for your direct report is also being processed.
4. You might be the second choice, and the HR team is waiting to hear from their first choice, who might not accept the job.
5. The firm is considering you for a different position based on your interview results, and they need to get that processed and cleared as well.
6. The person with final decision-making authority is away or ill.

PRACTICAL TIPS AND STRATEGIES

1. Maintain an active job search; don't put all your hopes on one interview.
2. Use the waiting period to upskill, especially in areas that may have seemed lacking during the interview.
3. Network actively, both online and offline, to keep abreast of new opportunities and insights.
4. Improve your LinkedIn account by engaging others and posting articles that attract the attention of others.
5. Volunteer work can provide a sense of purpose and add value to your resume.
6. Engage in activities that promote well-being, like starting a new hobby or an exercise routine.
7. Reflect on the interview to identify areas for improvement and act on them.

8. Reflect on how each proactive step, no matter how small, brings you closer to where God intends you to be. Trust in his timing, and remember, your worth is not defined by your job status but by your relationship with him.

CALL-TO-ACTION

Review your post-interview strategy. Are there areas you could improve upon or activities you haven't yet tried? Plan to incorporate these into your routine as you await the next steps in your job search.

Be faithful and trust that God is working on your behalf. If this position is meant for you, it will happen. Patience. Keep moving. Set up other interviews and continue to do your best. While he was imprisoned, Apostle Paul sent a letter to the Christians in Philippi, reassuring them of the peace and calm of Christ. He was expressing his gratitude and appreciation for their trust and belief for the mission work he began. He reminded them not to be fearful or anxious about anything.

"Do not be anxious about anything, but in every situation, by prayer and petition, with thanksgiving, present your requests to God. And the peace of God, which transcends all understanding, will guard your hearts and your minds in Christ Jesus."
Philippians 4:6–7 (NIV)

CLOSING PRAYER

Heavenly Father, grant us the patience to wait for your timing and the wisdom to use our waiting time wisely. As we seek your will for our professional lives, help us remain proactive, positive, and faithful, knowing you are working behind the scenes for our good.

MY TAKE AWAYS

_____

_____

_____

_____

_____

_____

_____

_____

_____

_____

_____

_____

21

PLEASE DON'T CALL THE EMPLOYER TO ASK IF YOU GOT THE JOB

"Destiny is not for comfort seekers. Destiny is for the daring and determined who are willing to at times endure some discomfort, delayed gratification, and go where destiny leads."
Bishop TD Jakes

Ring, ring, ring…. "Hi, my name is Jack Smith, and I interviewed for a job last week. I'm calling to see if I got the job. I think someone forgot to call me." Click.

In the journey of job seeking, the ticking of the clock can be the loudest sound in a room filled with anticipation. The period of waiting to hear back from a potential employer post-interview is a test of patience, a virtue highly valued yet challenging to master. This chapter will explore the discipline of patience and its integral role in the job search process, offering guidance on navigating the silent gaps between interviews with grace and purpose.

Waiting after an interview can seem eternal, yet it often spans only a few business days. Contacting an employer too soon to inquire about your status can be a misstep, potentially damaging your candidacy. *Patience is not merely a passive waiting but an active engagement in faith and trust.* There's a divine orchestration in our lives, where not receiving immediate feedback does not equate to a denial from God but an invitation to trust in his timing and plan.

Various unseen reasons may contribute to an employer's silence, such as unsecured funding for the position, ongoing interviews, or internal deliberations. These are external factors beyond one's control and should not be internalized as personal failures. Instead, this period should be embraced as an opportunity to demonstrate resilience and trust in the process, both human and divine.

During my career, I have witnessed the anxiety that accompanies the waiting phase. I've learned to perceive this not as idle time but as a moment for reflection, growth, and preparation for what lies ahead. When no response is received, wait and see. Consider it a redirection rather than a rejection, a guiding hand steering you toward where you are meant to be. Sending a thoughtful follow-up email a week post-interview can gently remind employers of your interest and candidacy. This communication should be courteous and professional, expressing gratitude for the opportunity to interview, and should not pressure for a decision. Instead, it serves as a gentle nudge, a reminder of your continued interest and presence.

Job searching requires grit. If you have the grit needed, you have the endurance to be patient and eventually take that next step when offered. As I have stated in other segments, if you have done your best and all that is possible, then it's time for you to just wait. Allow God the time to handle the rest. If you are not the candidate selected, it does not mean God did not answer your prayers. God is not a vending machine where you put in a prayer request, and out comes your answered prayer. God is working on your behalf to achieve what he designed for you. If it's not this job, it means another job is waiting for you. The biblical narrative is chock full of instances of waiting, reflecting a deep trust in God's providence. Paul the apostle, in his letters, encouraged patience and faith in the face of uncertainty, echoing the sentiments we must harbor as we navigate the unknowns of job hunting.

Every candidate deserves to be treated professionally and with proper protocol. If, in fact, you receive a rejection notice, you can choose to ask for feedback that will help you with future interviews. A template email might say:

> Dear...
> Thank you for taking the time to notify me of your final decision. It was an honor to meet the team and be considered as a candidate. If you would oblige, I would greatly appreciate

some feedback on my interview responses and how I can possibly improve my performance for future interviews. I know this means sacrificing some of your time. As a person seeking to always grow and improve, I would greatly appreciate the opportunity to hear from you. Thank you for your time and effort.

Sincerely,

However, it does not mean they will comply with your request. For most employers, it's a matter of you weren't selected, so there's no need for them to continue a conversation with you. It's not advisable to place all your hopes in one position, so keep pursuing your job search. Be patient. Be humble. Waiting on the Lord stretches our faith muscles and makes us stronger.

PRACTICAL TIPS AND STRATEGIES

1. Exercise patience and self-control by not rushing to follow up immediately after an interview.
2. Utilize the waiting time to reflect on the interview and identify areas for self-improvement.
3. Continue to apply for other positions and engage in professional development.
4. Should you decide to follow up, ensure your communication reflects a tone of gratitude, not desperation or impatience.

5. Reflect on the reasons you may not have heard back and use this time wisely to prepare for future opportunities. Consider the ways in which you can maintain a spirit of gratitude and trust, even when outcomes are uncertain.

CALL-TO-ACTION

If you're in a waiting phase, take a proactive step today. Review your resume, reach out to a network contact, or learn a new skill relevant to your career path. Every action you take is a seed planted for future success.

Our Bible is filled with stories of great patience. Women like Sarah, Rebekah, Hannah, and Rachel all waited patiently and trusted God, even though it seemed impossible for them to conceive a child. Esther ascended to the throne of Persia after waiting patiently for the right time to defeat Haman. She waited for God to make her move. So will you as you lean into God's wisdom.

"The end of a matter is better than its beginning, and patience is better than pride."
Ecclesiastes 7:8 (NIV)

CLOSING PRAYER

Lord, grant us the patience to wait, the strength to trust your timing, and the faith to believe you are working behind the scenes for our good. May we rest in your promises and remain steadfast in hope, knowing what you meant for us will not pass us by.

MY TAKE AWAYS

_____

_____

_____

_____

_____

_____

_____

_____

_____

_____

_____

_____

_____

22

ANCHORED BY COMMUNITY: CONSTRUCT YOUR SUPPORT SYSTEM

"Ask for help not because you are weak but because you want to remain strong."
Les Brown

T he journey through unemployment can be an isolated road or a path teeming with support. It's so important that we highlight the need for you to create a support system that not only sustains you through the trials of joblessness but also enriches your spirit and character.

In the stillness of unemployment, I've learned support is not a luxury; it is a necessity. A robust support system is a tapestry of encouragers, mentors, friends, and faith, woven together to hold you up when the ground beneath you seems to give way. It's the friend who listens without judgment, the mentor who offers wisdom, the community that prays with you, and the family that extends a hand in times of need.

The most important suggestion I have about your support system is *you identify a truth teller.* This is a person who keeps it real for you and helps you along with being honest and guides you, especially when you might be in denial or just don't want to listen to anyone. This truth teller has your permission to be honest with you while you wallow in discouragement.

In addition to a truth teller and a supportive family, you might consider a small group. If you aren't familiar with the term "Small Group," many churches have these groups that operate within their structure to help everyone. Churches usually do not require membership or even attendance at their church to be a part of their small groups. These groups meet weekly/bi-weekly and go through Bible studies together, have community together, party together, cry together, and support each other. Small groups become like your extended family, and there is so much love and wisdom shared within the small group structure. I encourage you to join a small group at your local church. Many Bible verses remind us of the importance of a support system.

PRACTICAL TIPS AND STRATEGIES

1. Cultivate relationships with those who uplift you.
2. Engage with professional networks and mentors for guidance.
3. Find solace in spiritual communities and small groups.

4. Lean on family and friends for emotional and sometimes financial support.
5. Stay connected with your faith through prayer and having community with others.
6. Reflect on the strength of your current support system. Does it reflect the diverse needs of your journey? Are you open to receiving help, and equally, are you willing to offer support to others?

CALL-TO-ACTION

Take a step today to strengthen or build one aspect of your support system. Reach out for professional guidance, join a new community group, or simply call a friend.

> "Two are better than one, because they have a good return for their labor: If either of them falls down, one can help the other up. But pity anyone who falls and has no one to help them up."
> Ecclesiastes 4:9–10 (NIV)

CLOSING PRAYER

Heavenly Father, we thank you for the gift of fellowship and community. May we always find the support we need in your love and in the companionship of others. Help us also to be a beacon of support to those in need.

MY TAKE AWAYS

_____

_____

_____

_____

_____

_____

_____

_____

_____

_____

_____

_____

FINISHING
IT ALL UP

23

CURATING A POSITIVE SOCIAL MEDIA PRESENCE

"It takes many good deeds to build a good reputation, and only one bad one to lose it."
Benjamin Franklin

n today's digital age, your online presence can speak volumes before you even utter a single word. This chapter guides you in aligning your social media profiles with the integrity and passion you embody, ensuring they reflect the best version of yourself and your commitment to making a positive impact.

Once, I encountered a bright candidate whose social media presence nearly cost them a dream role. Despite their qualifications, their online profiles painted a picture of their less discerning days. It's a stark reminder that our online personas are extensions of ourselves and, indeed, a mirror into our characters.

As you curate your digital presence, consider it an extension of your resume—a platform showcasing your growth, values, and contributions to causes you care deeply about. It's not just about erasing the past but about building a presence that speaks to your integrity and the positive influence you aim to be. If you're looking for tips, possibly consider looking at social media accounts of people who possess a moral compass and live lives of integrity. Do your posts reflect your passions and causes that would be an advantage to your profile? When you demonstrate the quality of compassion serving a higher cause to help others, you're enlightening others about your sense of commitment.

Also remember you can use social media for job seeking too. Many companies now use it to highlight their openings. They know recruitment through social media is very effective because they know most probably you spend a decent amount of time on your phone as well. Companies are also checking out your profiles (even though they are not supposed to use this method for judging you) to see what your skills level is, how savvy you are in promoting your own brand, and whether it aligns with theirs. If your profiles are appropriate and highlight you well, be sure to share them with employers and recruiters.

In our walk of faith, we are taught the importance of integrity—that our actions in both public and private life should reflect kindness and compassion. In a similar vein, *your social media should echo the principles you stand for,* demonstrating your commitment to living a life that honors those values.

PRACTICAL TIPS AND STRATEGIES

1. Audit your online profiles regularly to ensure they are in line with the image you wish to project professionally and personally.
2. Actively contribute to discussions and causes that resonate with your values and professional interests.
3. Be mindful of the content you share and engage with, ensuring it positively contributes to your personal brand and communicates integrity.

CALL-TO-ACTION OR NEXT STEPS

Review your social media accounts today. Remove what doesn't serve you and cultivate a presence that truly represents who you are and who you aspire to be.

Reflect on the content that fills your timelines and feeds— does it reflect the causes you champion? Does it mirror a life led by faith and purpose? Let these questions guide you as you sculpt your online narrative.

"In the same way, let your light shine before others, that they may see your good deeds and glorify your Father in heaven."
Matthew 5:16 (NIV)

CLOSING PRAYER

Lord, guide us as we navigate the digital realm. Help us be lights in the virtual community, showcasing the gifts you have given us guided by a life of faith and integrity. May our profiles demonstrate the work you are doing in our lives and encourage others to seek the goodness within their own paths.

MY TAKE AWAYS

_____

_____

_____

_____

_____

_____

_____

_____

_____

_____

_____

_____

_____

24

OVERCOMING FEAR

Some heart surgery takes a lifetime.

I t lurks in the shadows of our ambitions, whispering doubts and weaving tales of failure in our hearts. It stops us from moving forward with many decisions that could have changed our lives and filled our future with opportunities. What has such power? *Fear only has the power that we give it.* Navigating the treacherous waters of a career path can often feel like an odyssey where fear is the most formidable monster we must slay. My journey, like so many others, has been dotted with these encounters where fear seemed an insurmountable giant.

I remember vividly standing at the cusp of a significant career decision. It was an opportunity that could propel me into a future bright with promise, yet it was shrouded in the mist of the unknown. As I stood there, fear became tangible, an icy grip on my heart, questioning my qualifications, my readiness, and my faith. It's in these moments I realized fear could either be a barrier or a gateway to growth, depending on my response.

In times of career uncertainty, like preparing for an interview, fear can have a crippling effect. We imagine a thousand scenarios of failure. Our speech may become a gallop, our pauses oceans of silence. But it was in one such moment of trepidation where I found an anchor in the storm—a Scripture passage that reminded me of a love that casts out fear, a power given to me that was not of timidity but of strength.

There's a humbling beauty in acknowledging our fear, not as a sign of weakness but as a testament to our humanity. It's in this vulnerability that we find our greatest strength through faith. *"Some heart surgery takes a lifetime."* As we venture on the rollercoaster ride of indecision, we are constantly given opportunities for God to work on our hearts. By surrendering our fears to God, we open ourselves to his guidance and the possibilities He has in store for us—possibilities that far exceed the confines of our trepidation.

The apostle Paul's struggle with fear as he sat in his prison cell resonates with those of us who have faced the isolation that fear can bring. In his letter to Timothy, his spiritual son, he speaks of a divine inheritance of power, love, and self-discipline. This triad became my beacon, guiding me through the fog of fear and reminding me that I am not alone in my journey.

In career development, this inheritance translates into a boldness to pursue our vocation with vigor, to speak with confidence in interviews, and to make decisions not out of fear but out of faith. *We learn to differentiate between the healthy fear that sharpens our instincts and the destructive fear that erodes our spirit.*

I have learned every interview is not just a chance to negotiate a job offer but an opportunity to witness the interplay of divine providence and human preparation. I engage in a silent dialogue with God, a request for wisdom to speak not just with eloquence but with the truth of my character and the passion of my calling.

This divine dialogue continued beyond the interview space. It became a daily connection where each step in my career was a step taken with God. Whether it was navigating office politics, deciding on a promotion, or even when to step away from a role, this spiritual walk has illuminated paths once hidden by the darkness of fear. You control what your mind chooses to focus on. I want to see you succeed with basic tips you may not know. My purpose here is to encourage you to learn what you can, apply it, and trust God for it.

Are you letting fear control your life right now? Is there a dream you have that you must pursue but are too scared to even think of it happening? *Fear and doubt are dream killers.* Pray to God and talk to him about this dream. He wants to hear about it directly from you. Think about how many lost opportunities have passed you by because you thought it was not within your reach, personally and professionally. Often, I have heard my pastor at church say, "God does not call the equipped. He equips the called." You don't have to have it all ready. Trust God for the help you will need.

PRACTICAL TIPS AND STRATEGIES

1. Frame every career challenge as an opportunity for spiritual growth and professional development.

2. Use fear as a signal to engage in deeper reflection and prayer, seeking discernment for the next steps.

3. Create a "fear journal" to document your fears and the outcomes of situations where you have trusted God, observing patterns and celebrating victories over fear.

4. Contemplate how your career journey has been shaped by fear and how it could transform with a deeper integration of faith. How can you use your experiences to encourage others in their career pursuits?

CALL-TO-ACTION

Identify a career goal that seems out of reach due to fear. Craft a plan of action that includes both practical steps and spiritual practices to address this fear. Share this goal and plan with a trusted friend or mentor for accountability and support.

> "So we fix our eyes not on what is seen, but on what is unseen, since what is seen is temporary, but what is unseen is eternal."
> 2 Corinthians 4:18 (NIV)

CLOSING PRAYER

Heavenly Father, in the face of career fears, I seek the power, love, and self-discipline you promised. May my steps be bold and my path be clear, as I trust in your timing and your plan. In every decision, guide me with your wisdom and fill me with your peace.

MY TAKE AWAYS

_____

_____

_____

_____

_____

_____

_____

_____

_____

_____

_____

_____

25

LEARNING ZONES: THE GROWTH BEYOND COMFORT

"What lies behind us and what lies before us are
small matters compared to what lies within us."
Ralph Waldo Emerson

n this chapter, we delve into the transformative journey from comfort through learning to growth. Lev Vygotsky's insights into our learning zones provide a roadmap for this journey, showing how to embrace the unfamiliar and turn challenges into opportunities for personal and professional development.

There was a time in my career, much like Vygotsky's learning theory suggests, where my comfort zone was my refuge. But comfort, I learned, is often a prelude to complacency.

I recall a presentation sprung on me with scant minutes to prepare. Panic struck, but in that trial of necessity I found growth. This is the journey from panic to learning, where stretching beyond our perceived limits leads us to newfound competence.

Such was the case every time I faced a room of expectant faces, waiting for my words to guide them with unexpected presentations. The panic zone was where my resolve was tested, and the learning zone was where I honed my craft. It was the same for the biblical disciples, stepping into unknown towns tasked with spreading a transformative message. I can only imagine their reaction when Jesus dispersed them to spread the gospel and heal others. I'm sure they, too, went from comfort to panic, and as their belief grew, they, too, crept into the comfort zone somehow. They leaned not on their own understanding but on the divinely imparted wisdom and resilience granted to them.

The point of learning about the Learning Zones is so you can become more aware of your own behaviors, trials, successes, and failures and recognize them to improve yourself. Too many of us resort to staying in our comfort zones because of challenging experiences we do not want to relive. When you LIVE in your comfort zone and not just VISIT, you miss opportunities that may bring you a great sense of fulfillment. Can you imagine if you never got back on the bike or back in the driver's seat of your car or in any situation where you were not confident? Look at what you might have missed. This is so true with relationships also. Not going there today; that's another book!

PRACTICAL TIPS AND STRATEGIES

1. Recognize your comfort zone and the signs you are retreating to it.
2. Consciously step into new experiences to broaden your learning zone.
3. When facing panic, focus on what you can control and use practiced skills to stabilize your thoughts.
4. Reflect on past experiences where you've successfully navigated from panic to learning.
5. Consider the last time you were thrust out of your comfort zone. How did it feel? What did you learn? Reflect on how these experiences shaped your approach to new challenges.
6. Pray for the courage to step into your learning zone and trust that, like the disciples, you are equipped for the journey ahead.

CALL-TO-ACTION

Challenge yourself this week to take on a task that lies just outside your comfort zone. Embrace the initial discomfort as a sign of impending growth.

God always goes before us. Honor him and trust him for all your needs. One day, it will be for a successful job interview that leads to a new career, and the next day, you will seek him for a good annual check-up. He handles it all.

Then Jesus said to his disciples: "Therefore I tell you, do not worry about your life, what you will eat; or about your body, what you will wear. For life is more than food, and the body more than clothes. Consider the ravens: They do not sow or reap; they have no storeroom or barn; yet God feeds them. And how much more valuable you are than birds! Who of you by worrying can add a single hour to your life? Since you cannot do this very little thing, why do you worry about the rest? Consider how the wildflowers grow. They do not labor or spin. Yet I tell you, not even Solomon in all his splendor was dressed like one of these. If that is how God clothes the grass of the field, which is here today, and tomorrow is thrown into the fire, how much more will he clothe you—you of little faith!"
Luke 12:22–28 (NIV)

CLOSING PRAYER

Lord, guide us through our learning zones, from the first uncertain steps to the assurance of growth. Help us trust in the wisdom you provide, knowing each challenge is an opportunity to extend the borders of our capabilities, much like the disciples who trusted in your Word and spread your teachings across the lands.

THE LEARNING ZONES

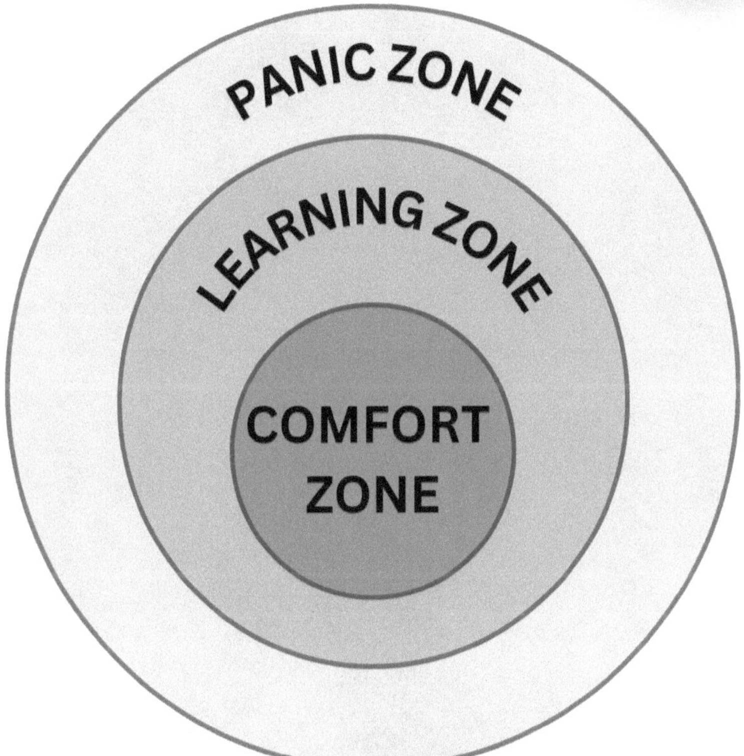

PANIC ZONE

LEARNING ZONE

COMFORT ZONE

*THE THEORY OF THE LEARNING ZONES WAS DEVELOPED
BY LEV VYGOTSKY, PSYCHOLOGIST

*Vygotsky, L.S. (1978). Mind in society: The development of higher psychological processes Cambridge, Mass.: Harvard University Press.

MY TAKE AWAYS

_____

_____

_____

_____

_____

_____

_____

_____

_____

_____

_____

_____

RESILIENCE: RISING AFTER REJECTION

"The trouble with most of us is that we would rather be ruined by praise than saved by criticism."
Norman Vincent Peale

R ejection is an inevitable companion on the path to professional fulfillment. It challenges our resilience, questions our abilities, and often leaves us with self-doubt. However, it's not the rejection itself but how we respond to it, that defines our character. Please remember if you have experienced a rejection, it's about your alignment with this job and not a statement of you as a person. *This chapter seeks to guide you through the process of turning the sting of job rejection into a catalyst for growth and self-confidence. In other words, opportunity has arrived.*

During my years as a career coach, I have witnessed

many faces clouded with the despair of rejection. Hearing stories from many during the 2008 recession is what motivated me to start helping people with this process. The success job seekers faced as I helped them is also what motivated me to create a comprehensive class I taught in my church in New York and here on the West Coast. I recall my experiences when I faced the cold silence after an interview, which I thought went well. Each silence, each polite refusal, was a test of faith, a moment to either succumb to despair or to look upward for strength.

One particular episode etched in my memory is when I was vying for a role that seemed tailor-made for my skills. The rejection was abrupt, leaving a void of confusion and self-doubt. However, in this moment of vulnerability, I was reminded of Jeremiah 29:11, which speaks of plans for prosperity and not harm, for a future filled with hope. Embracing this, I shifted my gaze from the closed door to the possibilities that lay ahead. *This was not a derailment but a redirection from God, a divine nudge toward a path better suited for the unique blueprint He crafted within me.*

The journey from rejection to resilience is paved with lessons. Here are strategies forged from both personal and observed experiences:

1. Identify and challenge negative self-talk. Ask yourself…. is it true?
2. Set realistic goals and celebrate small victories.
3. View mistakes as learning opportunities.

4. Cultivate skills and competence through continuous learning.
5. Surround yourself with positivity and support.
6. Take care of your physical and mental well-being.
7. Visualize success and affirm your potential.
8. Embrace professional help if self-doubt persists.

POSSIBLE REASONS WHY YOU WERE REJECTED

1. You may have the knowledge and ability, but you may not have the disposition they are looking for. It doesn't mean you can't do the job. Perhaps they are looking for a more social candidate, perhaps a more reserved candidate.
2. It may be the employee presently working in the position changed their mind and is no longer leaving the firm. They may or may not share this with you.
3. Perhaps the employee presently working in the firm was asking for an increase, which was not possible at the time, but the funding was found to keep that employee.
4. Have you considered the position was advertised before the funding for the position was fulfilled?
5. Maybe the person who was a previous choice before you interviewed changed their mind and accepted the position.
6. Perhaps the project which you were going to lead got scrapped.

7. Maybe your direct report already had someone in mind for the position and preferred that person.

8. It's very possible you impressed them so much that they want to consider you for a different position that has not been finalized yet.

I can literally go on and on. We may never know the reason or causes which moved the firm to the decision they made in not accepting you.

Now, here is a list of how to improve your chances if you were rejected for a position

Self-reflection is a part of growth and maturity. Your ability to proactively do this on a regular basis and own the parts of a situation that may have gone wrong is a true sign of your leadership and humility. Everyone has room for growth. Not only is it necessary to grow in any role you have at work, but it's also very attractive to employers. Who wants to work with a know-it-all?

LET'S CONSIDER THESE THINGS FOR IMPROVEMENT

1. Are you able to demonstrate qualities of humility and integrity during the interview?

2. Do you get caught up in having difficulty answering the same question every time you are interviewed? If you are, what are you doing to prepare a better answer for the next interview?

3. Are you participating in mock interviews with someone?

4. Are you speaking from the heart, or are you sounding robotic and rehearsed?

5. Are you preparing your interview answers based on the level of the interview?

6. Are you owning mistakes and working on not repeating them?

7. Are you dressed too casual or too formal?

8. Were you too aggressive or too relaxed?

9. Do you prepare great questions that demonstrate your passion and interest in the company?

10. Are you remembering to humble yourself in prayer?

11. Can you speak confidently without sounding arrogant?

12. Did you do your research about the company?

13. God has a better opportunity waiting for you one or two more rejections away.

14. Are you possibly setting yourself up for failure with unrealistic expectations?

PRACTICAL TIPS AND STRATEGIES

Moving forward from rejection requires actionable steps. Here are strategies to regain your confidence:

1. Take time to introspect. What can you learn from this experience? How can you improve for the next opportunity?

2. Analyze your resume, cover letter, and interview techniques. Seek feedback and make necessary adjustments.

3. Use this time to enhance your skills or learn new ones. Consider online courses, workshops, or reading material relevant to your field.
4. Build relationships within your industry. Attend events, join online forums, and connect with professionals on platforms like LinkedIn.

Remember, rejection is not a reflection of your worth. Each "no" is a step closer to the "yes" that will change your life. Consider journaling your thoughts and prayers, seeking clarity and peace as you trust in God's plan for your professional life.

CALL-TO-ACTION

Today, reach out to a mentor or trusted friend to discuss your career aspirations and the recent rejection. Gain insights and plan your next steps with their guidance.

There's a story in the book of Matthew when Jesus was traveling to Jerusalem with the disciples, and he saw a fig tree on the side of the road. The fig tree was dry and bore no fruit. Upon cursing the fig tree to never bear fruit again, the tree withered up. The disciples were amazed and asked Jesus how that happened. The disciples followed Jesus, asking how he could curse the fig tree, and he revealed that anything we do in faith that lines up with God's plan for us will succeed. As discussed in other chapters, God does not grant wishes like a vending machine. Getting closer to him will help you understand his plan for you.

CLOSING PRAYER

Lord, in the face of rejection, let us find your guiding hand. Give us the grace to persevere and the wisdom to see your plan in every setback. May we emerge stronger, more skilled, and ready to embrace the opportunities you have in store for us.

MY TAKE AWAYS

27

EMBRACING THE BOUNCE: A STEPPING STONE TO SUCCESS

"A man who carries a cat by the tail learns something he can learn in no other way."
Mark Twain

We must confront the inevitable experience of rejection during job interviews, transforming what is often perceived as a setback into a stepping stone for growth and self-improvement. It offers insight into how rejection can be a catalyst for personal and professional development. Let's figure out how to bounce back together.

In the task of job searching, rejection can often feel like a personal indictment, a harsh judgment on one's capabilities. *Yet, it's in these moments of apparent failure when the seeds of success are sown.* The journey through my professional landscape has been punctuated with rejections, each one a lesson in disguise, prompting a deeper self-inquiry and realignment with my true calling. The echo of a "no" can resonate deeply, but it's what we choose to hear in that echo that defines our path forward. Please be open and honest with yourself. Denial of your need to change your approach does not lead to progress.

Understanding the nuances of rejection is an art in itself. It's not just about the immediate sting but also about the aftermath—how we pick ourselves up, bounce back, dust off the disappointment, and pivot toward new horizons. In the wake of rejection, I've found comfort in reflection, reliving each interview to extract great responses and pearls of wisdom from the goofs I should have kept to myself. This self-analysis is not for the faint of heart; it requires a candid look inward, an acknowledgment of one's shortcomings, and the humility to seek growth.

Let's consider the experience of Jesus, who faced relentless rejection despite his teachings and miracles. Even though the disciples witnessed some miracles, they often questioned how the next situation could lead to another miracle. His journey teaches us about the strength inherent in facing opposition. He embraced his path with a steadfast heart, unaffected by the scorn of others, illustrating our mission is not to be validated by external acceptance but to persist in the truth of our calling.

As we wade through the waters of rejection, it's essential

to remember our professional worth is not contingent upon the acceptance of others. It's a truth I've grappled with in my darkest hours, like during the recession of 2008, when job prospects seemed as barren as the winter trees. Yet, it was in this seemingly desolate landscape that I found my resolve, leaning not on my own understanding but on the unwavering belief there was a purpose to my journey.

Are you finding you are invited to first interviews but not to second-level follow-ups? After each interview, conduct a self-reflection analysis and determine which questions consistently trouble you so you can focus on developing those answers further. Scan the **QR code** in this section so you can download a free, easy-to-use template following each interview to do just that. Trust the process. It's a tried and true good one. Consider the time when you dated, and the first one didn't go well. Repeating the same behaviors and comments led to the same responses for a career of first-time dating. You eventually figured out how to get out of that cycle by changing something up. Interviews are very similar.

PRACTICAL TIPS AND STRATEGIES

1. Before the interview, set a clear intention for what you wish to convey and learn.
2. During the interview, remain present and attuned to the dynamics of the conversation.
3. After the interview, engage in a ritual of self-reflection, assessing both the tangible and intangible aspects of the exchange.

4. Embrace a holistic approach to rejection, seeing it not as a singular event but as part of a larger narrative of growth and self-discovery.

5. Cultivate a mindset that views each rejection as an opportunity to refine your professional narrative and clarify your career aspirations.

6. Reflect on the rejections we've faced. What stories have they told us about ourselves? How have they redirected our paths in ways we couldn't have anticipated? In the aftermath of rejection, there lies a profound opportunity for introspection and recalibration. It's a chance to fortify our faith, reassess our journey, and prepare ourselves for the doors that will open in due time.

CALL-TO-ACTION

Consider the last interview that didn't go in your favor. What can you learn from it? Create an action plan for the next interview, focusing on the areas you wish to improve. Embrace the growth that comes from each experience and move forward with confidence and faith.

When experiencing a rejection, don't allow negative behavior that will leave a permanent memory with someone during a period of your temporary life. Just remember to lean into God and trust him for your hopes, your career, and your future. In the apostle Paul's letter to the church of Corinth, he pleads for forgiveness and grace. Our strength grows in and through our weaknesses.

> *"But he said to me, 'My grace is sufficient for you, for my power is made perfect in weakness.' Therefore, I will boast all the more gladly about my weaknesses, so that Christ's power may rest on me."*
> 2 Corinthians 12:9 (NIV)

CLOSING PRAYER

Heavenly Father, in the face of rejection, let us find strength in your Word and comfort in your promises. Guide us to understand each "no" we encounter is not a dead end but a detour, leading us to your plans for our prosperity and purpose. In our weaknesses, reveal your power, and in our disappointments, show us your direction.

POST-INTERVIEW WORKSHEET

MY TAKE AWAYS

_____

_____

_____

_____

_____

_____

_____

_____

_____

_____

_____

_____

_____

28

THE GIFT OF SERVICE: UNEMPLOYMENT AS A TIME FOR GROWTH

"God has given us two hands, one to receive with and the other to give with."
Billy Graham

Staying positive while job seeking can be a daunting endeavor, as from day to day, it's accompanied by a rollercoaster of emotions. Hope, despair, hope, despair. Here, we invite you to consider how serving others can transform not only your career search but also your personal development and sense of fulfillment. You might think... help someone else when I need help? Yes, that's exactly what I said. And more importantly, it works because we will do what God created us to do...help others.

During my unemployment in the economic downturn in 2008, I turned to volunteering. This decision, while born out of a need to remain productive, became a journey of the return to self-discovery. I've volunteered in many places throughout my lifetime. However, when I sunk low, I thought only of myself. It's here, in the act of giving, that my burdens felt lighter, my purpose clearer, and my value was not tethered to a job title. As I extended my hand to help others, my path became more apparent—my purpose, once dormant, is to actively influence the lives of others with the gifts God has given me.

Volunteering became a beacon during my job interviews, a testament to my character and initiative. It's this altruistic engagement employers often admire, signifying a proactive, community-oriented, and adaptable candidate. The skills honed and the networks formed during these times often opened doors to unforeseen career opportunities.

When asked that familiar question during an interview, "How are you spending your time during unemployment?" I'm sure your answer should not be, "In a pity party, binging on chips and tacos and a lot of television so I could bury my discouragement."

How many times do you remember someone helping you even when you did not have the courage to ask for it? How secretly grateful were you? We all have moments of pridefulness and don't want to ask for help because we feel we need to prove we can do things on our own. *I am always grateful for the many people who have helped me in my lifetime, especially when I was too proud to ask.* God has stepped in on your behalf more times than you can count or realize by connecting you to those who can guide and help you.

Have you ever thought this is a great time for you to do some soul-searching to consider what your true passion is? There is a myth that everyone's career should be what their passion is. Often, this is not possible. A passion one has might not sustain you financially, and that's why this is a great time to go after your passion as a volunteer. I've created a way of helping you discover what that might be. Scan the **QR code** in this chapter and get busy.

PRACTICAL TIPS AND STRATEGIES

1. Seek volunteer opportunities that align with your skills and passion.
2. Incorporate your volunteer experiences into your resume and interviews.
3. Use the time spent volunteering to network and learn new skills.
4. Reflect on the benefits your service brings to both others and yourself.
5. Reflect upon your experiences with helping others. How have these moments shifted your perspective on your current circumstances? Consider how service can lead to unexpected opportunities. Embrace the humility and lessons learned through volunteerism and carry them forward into your career search and beyond.

CALL-TO-ACTION

Identify a local organization where your skills can benefit others. Commit to a period of service and note the ways it enriches your life and career search.

In the book of John, John the apostle reminds us Jesus wanted us to know how important it was for us to love each other and show each other compassion, kindness, and, above all, love. Jesus is the vine, and we are the branches attached to the vine. Alone, we cannot survive. Always connected to him, we will be nurtured, and we will bear fruit. The fruit he speaks of is the fruits of the spirit…kindness, patience, gentleness, faithfulness, and more.

> *"Greater love has no one than this: to lay down one's life for one's friends. You are my friends if you do what I command. I no longer call you servants because a servant does not know his master's business. Instead, I have called you friends, for everything that I learned from my Father I have made known to you. You did not choose me, but I chose you and appointed you so that you might go and bear fruit—fruit that will last—and so that whatever you ask in my name the Father will give you. This is my command: Love each other."*
> John 15:13–17 (NIV)

CLOSING PRAYER

Father, in our seasons of searching, help us remember the value of serving others. May we find joy and purpose in the act of giving and trust that through our service, you are molding us for the path ahead.

IDENTIFY YOUR PASSION AND PURPOSE

MY TAKE AWAYS

_____

_____

_____

_____

_____

_____

_____

_____

_____

_____

_____

_____

_____

29

AT THE CROSSROADS: IS IT TIME TO LEAVE YOUR JOB?

> "Transformation is a process, and as life happens
> there are tons of ups and downs. It's a journey of
> discovery—there are moments on mountaintops
> and moments in deep valleys of despair."
> Rick Warren

D eciding to leave a job, whether for a promotion, a new opportunity, or due to a challenging work environment, is a significant life transition that can bring both excitement and uncertainty. Here, we seek to guide you through these various scenarios, offering insights on how to approach this critical decision with wisdom and faith.

Navigating the complex emotions and practical considerations of leaving a job can be daunting. In my career coaching experience, I've seen individuals grapple with the joy of being sought after and the discomfort of outgrowing a once-cherished role. The Bible, in 1 Peter, speaks to the steadfastness of faith during life's changes, urging us to trust in God's plan.

When presented with a promotion that doesn't include a salary increase, the challenge is to weigh the value of the new responsibilities against the lack of financial reward. I've counseled clients through such decisions, reminding them to do their research and seek God's wisdom for clarity.

The temptation and ego satisfaction of being recruited by another firm can be strong, yet it's vital to look beneath the surface. I've seen individuals leap at such chances, only to find themselves in roles that were not as they seemed. Thus, it is important to question and listen to one's intuition, trusting God will lead you to where your gifts can be best utilized.

IF YOU ARE FACING A POTENTIAL OPPORTUNITY, CONSIDER THESE QUESTIONS:

1. Why did the person/s working in this position leave?
2. Is the leader of the new firm someone you will look up to and want to emulate?
3. Is it a great opportunity with many chances for growth and leadership?
4. How many people have filled this position in the past five years?
5. What is the turnover like at this firm?

6. Does your intuition tell you that you would be inheriting a lot of serious problems that are more than you can handle?

7. Are there perks that make up the difference of your preferred salary? These perks may include a company vehicle, tuition reimbursement, paid extended vacation time, the chance to transition to total remote status, reduced responsibilities, and the chance to lead a great team.

The toxicity in the workplace is a reality many face, and it's crucial to recognize when it's time to step away. The Bible doesn't call us to endure unhealthy environments but to seek peace and fulfillment. Sometimes, staying true to our path means having the courage to change course.

WHAT MAY LEAD TO A TOXIC WORK ENVIRONMENT

1. Competition is not healthy; it's actually antagonistic.
2. Leadership does not stand by their promises.
3. Colleagues are complaining about the overworked schedules and caseload.
4. Leadership does not show interest in your work or even their own.
5. Employees are underpaid, and previous salary commitments are not respected.
6. Change of leadership is executed with a poor transition.

7. Your contributions are not recognized.
8. Colleagues are always receiving preferential treatment and increases.

When personal growth stalls, it's a sign we may need to seek new challenges. I've witnessed the transformation in individuals who have taken the bold step to leave a job, trusting God has a plan for their growth and happiness.

POTENTIAL QUESTIONS TO ASK YOURSELF IF YOU ARE EXPERIENCING A LACK OF GROWTH:

1. Have you made consistent achievements as part of your contribution?
2. Are you losing interest?
3. Have your passions or ideas about what you wanted changed?
4. Have you been overlooked for opportunities?
5. Is leadership not showing the interest you had hoped for?
6. Has the firm changed leadership, and has the structure shifted?

PRACTICAL TIPS AND STRATEGIES

1. Reflect on the reasons for considering a job change; weigh these against your long-term career goals.

2. Consider the potential for growth and learning in the new role versus the current one.

3. Pray and seek God's guidance, remembering his plans are to prosper you, not to harm you.

4. Contemplate your current job situation. Are you growing? Are you valued? Does the environment enable you to thrive? Use these reflections to assess whether a change aligns with the career growth you seek and the life God intends for you.

CALL-TO-ACTION

List the pros and cons of your potential job change. Seek counsel from trusted mentors and lay the decision before God in prayer, asking for guidance and confirmation.

Pray about your circumstances and ask God for the guidance you need before making a rushed decision. Consider short-term and long-term impacts. Have you got any coals in the fire before moving on?

"Forget the former things; do not dwell on the past. See, I am doing a new thing! Now it springs up; do you not perceive it? I am making a way in the wilderness and streams in the wasteland."
Isaiah 43:18–19 (NIV)

CLOSING PRAYER

Heavenly Father, in times of decision, I seek your face. Grant me the wisdom to discern the path you have laid out for me and the courage to walk it, whether it means staying or leaving. Guide me in your truth and help me trust in your plan.

MY TAKE AWAYS

_____

_____

_____

_____

_____

_____

_____

_____

_____

_____

_____

_____

_____

30

COMPASSION: THE VALUE OF VOLUNTEERING IN TIMES OF TRANSITION

God: "Knock knock."
You: "Who's there?"
God: "Opportunity."
You: "Opportunity who?"
God: "Opportunity who may not come around again."
You: "How do I know if you are the right opportunity?"
God: "...Here we go again!"

Let's have a serious talk about opportunity. What does opportunity look like? It's usually not labeled for you. It doesn't have a neon sign that says look at me. I'm not talking about the job that stares you in the face as a great opportunity. *It's often hidden because it takes your discernment and skills to recognize it.* Often, it's not direct, either. In other words, it doesn't say if you do this, this will happen to you.

Great opportunities are what occur when you take action about something in faith, and, because of your faith, this great thing happens and opens the door to something bigger than you ever expected. In fact, opportunity usually yields rewards later when we least expect it. As I shared in another chapter, I always volunteered during a time of unemployment, which led to my next position more than once.

Times of unemployment are often seen as valleys in our professional journeys, yet they offer a fertile ground for growth, giving, and unrecognizable opportunities. This chapter explores the profound impact of volunteering during these transitions, not only for the communities we serve but also for our personal development and future employability.

I've always found comfort and fulfillment in volunteering, especially during my periods of transition. It's a time when your talents can shine in unexpected places, illuminating the paths of others while casting light on your own. The act of service reflects our compassionate Creator, who calls us to love and support each other, especially in times of need.

Volunteering bridges the gap between employment, providing purposeful engagement, and the joy of contributing to a cause greater than oneself. It's during these moments of selfless service that we often encounter new opportunities, learn new skills, and even cross paths with future employers.

Can you imagine sitting in an interview and the employer asks you, "So, Martin, I see you have a break in your career. How did you spend your time between 2022 and 2024 while you were unemployed?" And your response is, "Um…"

Wouldn't it be awesome to say, "I returned to school to acquire updated skills, and I also began volunteering, which brought me great fulfillment to make a difference for others who needed me? I really enjoyed helping other people during that time, and I continue to this day."? Doesn't this response feel wonderful? You were intentional about the opportunity to grow. Sadly, because some do not see this time as an opportunity, they opt for television binging with their favorite donuts.

Volunteering can also keep you engaged and grounded, and it allows you to interact with people so you can continue focusing on developing your social skills. Volunteering is a great way to network, and while you're volunteering, you just might meet the CEO of your next career move.

PRACTICAL TIPS AND STRATEGIES

1. Seek volunteer opportunities that resonate with your passions and utilize your skills.
2. Approach volunteering as a professional commitment, demonstrating your values and work ethic.
3. Use this time to network and build relationships that may lead to employment opportunities.
4. Reflect on how volunteering has enriched your life and consider how it could benefit your career trajectory. Have your service experiences introduced you to new networks or skill sets? Have they provided clarity on your professional calling?

CALL-TO-ACTION

You can volunteer in literally thousands of ways. Serve somewhere that aligns with your passion and tugs at your heart. My only suggestion when choosing a place is to select one that will absolutely consider your skills and the gifts God has given you. Your gifts from God should never go to waste. Identify a local organization aligned with your values. Consider this an investment in your community and your professional future.

> *"For I was hungry, and you gave me something to eat, I was thirsty, and you gave me something to drink, I was a stranger and you invited me in."*
> Matthew 25:35 (NIV)

CLOSING PRAYER

As we give of ourselves to help others, may we remember the blessings we have and the ability we possess to make a difference. May our actions be an example to the love we've received and the grace we are called to extend.

MY TAKE AWAYS

_____

_____

_____

_____

_____

_____

_____

_____

_____

_____

_____

_____

A FINAL WORD

I hope you have been able to extract many techniques and strategies that have helped countless others. More importantly, I hope you have gained new insight into how to think like the employer to formulate your thoughts and responses so that you can offer your best through your resumes and interviews. I'm looking forward to hearing how this handbook has helped and motivated you to seek out the best in you that God created you to become. If you have found this handbook helpful, please share your copy with someone you know who is experiencing the same struggle. Sharing wisdom can be a priceless gift.

If you'd like more information, strategies, and tips, please connect with me at <u>marshatom.com</u>. I have free, helpful templates for you to download, which will guide you through many challenges you might be facing. More importantly, I'm always ready to pray over your job interviews; just fill out the request online.

If you have experienced several first-level interviews with no follow-ups or if you feel coaching is something you would like to consider, it would be my honor to become the coach who can inspire you, help you grow, and reach the success you are seeking. Feel free to check out my website, so you can sign up for a free consultation. You can also read some testimonies about my coaching services below.

*****

TESTIMONIES

As a pharmacist who worked in the retail setting for years, I was suddenly presented with an opportunity to apply for my dream position at a hospital pharmacy. As a pharmacy manager, I had interviewed and hired numerous people; however, I was unfamiliar with going through the interview process. When Marsha met with me, I could see these were some of the most informative hours I have ever had. I learned so much from her during our sessions, and I knew exactly what to do and say for my actual interview. A lot of what I thought was appropriate to say during an interview were actually red flags that Marsha pointed out I needed to avoid. Marsha guided me throughout the meeting, and afterward, I felt ready and confident. Needless to say, I landed my dream job as Marsha prepared me well. Throughout the whole interview process, she was constantly following up with me. As a career coach, Marsha cares for the success of her clients; she puts other people's needs before her own, which makes her a very effective and caring coach. There is no one else I would trust my career with but Marsha.

Dung Nguyen, Outpatient Pharmacy Lead
SHARP Healthcare

Through Marsha's coaching, I was inspired to stretch my courage and tackle fears. She taught me so many things I would never have considered to share and some things not to share. I learned from her how to engage people in meaningful ways. With Marsha, it's always an upward mindset and a growth-oriented mindset. Since Marsha's coaching, I've now re-envisioned and achieved my top goals. Marsha's coaching has been pivotal in my career development as well as honing lifelong skills such as communication, public speaking, goal setting, planning, and execution of events.

Brianna Fox, Registered Behavior Technician
Action Behavior Centers

I had the benefit of participating in a career-building course and being personally coached by Marsha Tom. Marsha's expertise in creating a compelling resume and honing interview skills was evident from the very beginning of her course through her excellent, approachable, and engaging curriculum. During the course, she taught me fundamental principles in resume building, applying for jobs, and interviewing. What I appreciated most about Marsha was her personalized approach to career building and personal branding. She took the time to understand my specific needs and tailored her coaching to fit my goals.

Thanks to Marsha's coaching and the principles learned through this course, I was able to land my dream job as a manager of a ServiceNow development team. I highly recommend anything Marsha offers as you seek to build a fulfilling and thriving career if you are looking to stand out in the job market and ace your interview process.

Robert Melchor, Manager of ServiceNow Development SailPoint

Marsha's coaching took my job readiness through the gauntlet, and it immediately provided impact. Her sessions have great universal Do's and Don'ts, but she also takes the time to refine the process specifically for you. She'll structure the prep for your industry, prepare you for all types of interviews (phone interviews, video, in-person, panel interviews, behavioral and technical), and will identify important things to do before, during, and after each step.

Most importantly to me, Marsha values integrity in how she presents herself and wants her clients to do the same. I always want to be honest. I don't embellish my resume or sweep weaknesses under the rug, which made it hard to get a job (because I really didn't have much experience). Marsha taught me how to not only own up to my weaknesses in a non-detrimental way, but also how to leverage them to highlight my character, instead.

Marsha wants you to understand what you are doing; she wants you to feel confident going in, and she wants to lead you to the solution, not feed you the answer. It's not a cookie-cutter session where you memorize and regurgitate premade responses during a hypothetical interview. It's a Rocky-style training montage, except you don't get to fast forward to the part where you are successful! Marsha's process is effective because it is thorough. She will make you work; her mock interviews will probably be harder than your actual interview, but you would much rather make the mistakes working with her than on the interview itself!

Within one month of finishing the workshop, my new and improved LinkedIn was already receiving hits from recruiters. Quickly, I landed a job where I was even able to bypass the two-year job experience requirement!

Anthuan Cruz, Clinical Lab Technician
Veracyte Inc.

Whether you are just entering the workforce or a seasoned professional ready to make a move, Marsha can guide you by motivating you to discover your better self. Her personalized approach to career development focused on my individual growth as well as my resume writing and interview skills. Being coached by her not only helps you with your career awareness and skills, but you'll discover that she prepares you for success in your purpose and new role.

Joe Shan, VP, Clinical Operations
Adcentrx Therapeutics

She taught me fundamental principles in resume building, applying for jobs, and interviewing. These principles helped me gain a deeper understanding of what hiring managers look for in top candidates and provided a framework on how to gain a competitive advantage in the job market.

Desiree Abell, Senior Subcontracts Administrator
Leonardo DRS

During a challenging period of job loss, Marsha became a pillar of support for me when we crossed paths. She not only introduced me to volunteering as a way of growing during unemployment, but she served as my coach to get me moving in the right direction. Joining one of her classes proved invaluable as I absorbed valuable lessons, fostering personal and professional growth. Marsha guided me in cultivating my motivation, resourcefulness, and confidence in my skills in preparation for interviews. Through her guidance, I've embraced my work and integrated faith into how I align my values with my career.

Grace Joya, Dealer Relationship Manager
Kinetic Advantage, LLC

Marsha is one of the very unique people who has exceptional business sense and deep experience, coupled with a passion for helping people see and develop their potential. She does this by investing in people in a mentorship style rather than a transactional manner.

She often has more faith in a person's ability to grow and reach their goals than the person initially might possess. Her ability to assess a situation quickly enables her to provide insight and guidance for one's personal growth. I've experienced this first-hand and have seen many other people experience the same.

Marsha is willing to speak the truth into a situation of a person's abilities. Where Marsha moves forward, other coaches tend to refrain. Her willingness to be honest in a valuable and caring manner sets her apart.

Chris Lien, President/Educational Consultant
Tutor Doctor

Marsha was able to help me navigate through the interview and job-searching process with ease by providing expert coaching and guidance. It was evident that she had a passion for helping me succeed and achieve my goals. Marsha knows the ins and outs of the hiring process and exactly what the hiring teams are looking for. She was able to take my resume to the next level and helped me prepare for difficult questions. There was no "easy" route with Marsha's mock interviews, and as a result, the real ones were a breeze. Being coached by Marsha has been a pivotal moment in my career and I wholeheartedly put my trust in her without hesitation. I am extremely grateful for her teachings and will carry all that I learned and experienced with me for life.

Luke Carreon, Development Associate
Invivoscribe, Inc.

ABOUT THE AUTHOR

She has walked in your shoes.

Through her own journey, Marsha has encountered the discouragements and hurdles that many face in their careers, from the daunting task of job hunting to the struggle of finding one's place in an often indifferent job market. Her ability to transform these challenges into stepping stones toward self-discovery and success is a testament to her resilience and character. Her handbook is more than just a guide; it's a reflection of her journey, offering solace and actionable advice to those who feel lost, undervalued, and uncertain about their future.

Having experienced the lowest of lows through depression, failures, and hopelessness, her faith transformed her and shaped her genuine desire to support individuals in finding purpose and fulfillment in their careers and beyond. Marsha has enjoyed the privilege of using her life to serve thousands and continues doing this through her calling in every chapter of this handbook. Following a formidable career, her passion for teaching career and leadership courses led to coaching individuals through marshatom.com. She uses her own life experiences to connect with readers, making her advice relatable and grounded in reality.

Marsha has served over 275 thousand families as a Borough Director in the New York City Department of Education, a nonprofit CEO, she has taught art and was even a CASAC (Credentialed Substance Abuse Counselor) for many years as well as many other journeys of learning. She has led teams of hundreds and served thousands with her encouraging but very direct and pragmatic guidance.